平行人生
Parallel Lives

新宮 晋 ＋ レンゾ・ピアノ
Susumu Shingu + Renzo Piano

SEIGENSHA

はじめに

本書では、大阪出身の芸術家・新宮晋とジェノヴァ出身の建築家・レンゾ・ピアノ、日本とイタリアを代表する二大巨匠のコラボレーション作品を紹介します。

二人は、関西国際空港（プロジェクト期間：1988−1994年）の国際建築コンペを機に出会いました。設計者として選ばれたレンゾ・ピアノが「風のアーティスト」として注目を集めていた新宮晋に「空気の流れを見えるようにしてくれないか」と依頼したのがその始まりです。

ピアノの建築は前衛的である一方で、建物の内と外の境界線を取り去り、その場所の風土との調和を重んじるとてもやさしいものです。風・光・水をテーマに作品制作を行ってきた新宮と国境を越えて共感し合い、今日に至る30年余の間に、実現しただけでも10を数えるプロジェクトをイタリア、日本、ギリシャ、アメリカの各地に完成させてきました。そして、今なお未来に向けたプロジェクトが進んでいます。本書では今年86歳を迎える新宮とピアノの未来のプロジェクトもあわせて紹介します。

タイトルの「平行人生 Parallel Lives（パラレル・ライブス）」は、1〜2世紀のギリシャの哲学者プルタルコスが、多数の共通した性格や人生を送った二人の偉人を比較した列伝のタイトルに由来します。巻末には、映像の分野で前衛的な活動を行ってきたイタリアのグループ、スタジオ・アッズーロが、二人のスケッチや設計図、作品写真をもとに制作した映像のグラフィックで加わって、夢と冒険に満ちた二人の創造の世界と煌めく交差の軌跡を表現し、彼らの作品を読みとくための新たな視座を与えてくれます。

本書の刊行におきましては、イタリア文化会館−大阪をはじめ、様々な関係者のご尽力をいただきました。関係各位に、厚く御礼申し上げます。

Foreword

This book presents collaborative works by two great creative masters representing Japan and Italy, sculptor Susumu Shingu from Osaka and architect Renzo Piano from Genoa.

Shingu and Piano came together as a result of the international competition to design the passenger terminal building for Kansai International Airport, a project Piano worked on from 1988 to 1994. Piano had been selected as the designer, and the collaboration began when he asked Shingu, who had built a reputation as a "sculptor of the wind," to create something that would "make the streams of air visible."

Piano's architecture is avant-garde, but also very accommodating, eliminating boundaries between inside and outside and prioritizing harmony with the natural environment of the location. Piano and Shingu, an artist who works with themes of wind, light, and water, have enjoyed mutual understanding and respect for each other across national borders. They have completed ten projects together in Italy, Japan, Greece, and America over the course of more than three decades, as well as many unbuilt projects. They continue to work together with an eye to the future. This book includes such future projects by Shingu and Piano, who both turn eighty-six this year.

The title *Parallel Lives* is taken from a series of writings by the first and second century Greek philosopher Plutarch, who produced biographies of luminaries of Greek and Roman times arranged in pairs to bring out the similarities of their personalities and their lives. At the back of the book are graphics from videos based on sketches, designs, and photographs of works by Piano and Shingu produced by the Italian group Studio Azzurro, known for its avant-garde video art. These graphics give expression to the duo's creative world of dreams and adventure and to the shining moments when their paths have come together, providing a new perspective for understanding their work.

We would like to express our sincere thanks to the Italian Cultural Institute in Osaka, as well as to the many others involved in this project who made this book possible.

目　次

Index

平行人生

1989年、大阪府豊能町の山奥にあったぼくのアトリエに、イタリアのジェノヴァから一本の電話があった。「この度ぼくたちの事務所が関西国際空港の国際コンペで選ばれて、レンゾ・ピアノが今度大阪に行くのだけれど、彼は新宮さんに会いたがっています」。

その数日後、約束通り大阪のヒルトン・ホテルのロビーで、長い図面のロールを脇に抱えて現れたレンゾに会った。英語で挨拶を交わした後、イタリア語を話せると言うと、彼は「マンマミーア！（何ということだ！）」と叫んだ。そして長年の友人のように打ち解けることが出来、たまたま同い年だということも分かった。

彼がぼくに頼みたかったのは、国際線出発ロビーの空調からの流れのことで、「私たちは美しい空気の流れをデザインすることに成功した。しかし残念なことに、誰もそれを見ることが出来ない。どうか最小限の装置で、見えるようにしてくれないか？」彼は建築雑誌なんかでぼくの仕事を見て、興味を持ってくれていたらしい。こんな魅力的な提案を、断る理由は何もなかった。ぼくたちは、空気の中を泳ぎ続ける魚のようなものが良いということで意見は一致した。でも、それではどんなものを？ どんな風に？ それが現在まで、35年以上にわたって続くやり取りの始まりだった。いつも条件は違っていた。だから答えが違っているのは当然のことで、いつも一からの挑戦だった。そのためにお互いある種の緊張感もあり、新鮮な関係が続けられたのだと思う。

ぼくたちに共通していたのは、「飾りものの付け足しのアートは必要ない。それが加わることでその空間に意味が生まれ、豊かになるものなら創り出そう」という考え方だった。

先日も誰かがレンゾに尋ねた。「そんなに長年いっしょに仕事をしていたら、色々問題も多いんじゃない？」と。レンゾは「いや全然問題はないよ。自分は測量技師だし、新宮は機械屋だからね」と答えた。

そんな言い方ってあるのか。それだけじゃあないと思うけれど。まあまだ二人でやるべきことはいっぱいある。

造形作家　新宮 晋

Parallel Lives

In 1989, I was at my atelier in the mountains of Toyono-cho, in Osaka Prefecture, when I received a phone call from Genova. "We've just won the international competition to design the Kansai International Airport, and Renzo Piano is about to revisit Osaka. While he's there, he would like to meet you."

We met a few days later, in the lobby of the Hilton Hotel in Osaka. Renzo had a long roll of drawings tucked under his arm, and he greeted me in English. When he discovered that I could speak Italian, he was delighted, exclaiming "Mamma mia!" After that, we chatted like long-lost friends, and as we were talking, we realized that we'd both been born the same year.

Renzo explained that he wanted to talk to me about the air conditioning for the International Departures Lobby at the new airport. "We've done a beautiful design for the flow of air through the lobby, but sadly, no-one can see it. Can you create minimal devices that will make the streams of air visible?" He had been interested in my work after seeing it in an architecture magazine or somewhere. There was no way I would pass up the chance to work on such an interesting project. We both thought it would be good to have something moving in the air, much like the movement of a fish that is constantly swimming. But what sort of thing? And how should it move? Discussing this project was the beginning of an association between us that has lasted for over thirty-five years. Every project that we worked on together had different requirements. That's why every solution is different—we started from step one each time. That adds a little spice, making each project a new challenge for each of us, and keeping our connection fresh.

One of the things we have in common is our way of thinking: There's no need for art that only adds decoration. It's worth creating art that gives meaning to and enriches a space.

Somebody recently said to Renzo "If you've been working together for so long, there must have been times when problems arose between you." His reply was "There have been no problems at all. I'm the surveyor and he's the mechanic."

That was a strange way of putting it. I think there's more to it than that. There are lots of things that we still need to do.

artist, **Susumu Shingu**

パリ事務所での対談 2018年　at RPBW Paris, 2018

凡 例

・本書は2023年7月13日(木)から9月14日(木)まで大阪中之島美術館で開催する
「Parallel Lives 平行人生 ― 新宮晋＋レンゾ・ピアノ」展の図録として刊行された。

・文章中、頻繁に登場するレンゾ・ピアノの事務所名 Renzo Piano Building Workshop
(レンゾ・ピアノ ビルディング ワークショップ)はRPBWとして短縮形を用いて表記した。また、
Fondazione Renzo Piano(フォンダツィオーネ・レンゾ・ピアノ)はFRPと略している。

・本書には展覧会出品以外の作品も収録する。従って実際の展示における順番や
出品番号とは一致しない。

・作品情報は原則として作者が提供するデータに基づいた。

・建築作品については、原則としてプロジェクト期間を(YYYY-YYYY年)として記載
している。

・作品名は《 》でくくり、建築名は原則として「 」でくくるが、なじみのある空港名や
一般によく知られた場所を表す場合や見出し等は例外とする。

・本文中の解説は、平井直子と前波豊が執筆した。平井のレンゾ・ピアノ建築に関する解説
は主としてRPBW提供のテキストに基づく。前波の解説は新宮晋氏への取材に基づく。

平井直子　　p.28, 38, 48, 54, 64, 68, 76, 86, 92, 102, 114右, 118右, 122右, 126右,
　　　　　　130右, 134右, 138, 141, 144, 148, 152, 156, 160, 164, 168, 170, 188右, 192

前波豊　　　p.30, 40, 50, 56, 66, 70, 78, 88, 94, 104, 114左, 118左, 122左, 126左,
　　　　　　130左, 134左, 188左

Notes

・This catalogue is published in association with the exhibition *Parallel Lives
−Susumu Shingu + Renzo Piano* at the Nakanoshima Museum of Art,
Osaka from July 13 to September 14, 2023.

・For the purposes of this catalogue, Renzo Piano's Renzo Piano Building Workshop
is abbreviated as "RPBW." Similarly, Fondazione Renzo Piano is abbreviated as "FRP."

・The catalogue includes works that were not included in the exhibition.
Consequently, the sequence of exhibits and the exhibit numbers in the exhibition
do not match the catalogue.

・Data concerning the works is normally based on information provided by the creators.

・Dates for built works are normally given as the year that work began on
design and the year of completion (YYYY-YYYY).

・Titles of works and architecture are given in italics. Italics may be omitted for
familiar names, and within headings.

・Commentary in the catalogue text is written by Naoko Hirai and Yutaka
Maenami. The commentary about Renzo Piano's architectures by Naoko Hirai
is based on texts provided by RPBW. The commentary by Yutaka Maenami is
based on interviews with Susumu Shingu.

Naoko Hirai　　　pp. 28, 38, 48, 54, 64, 68, 76, 86, 92, 102, 114r, 118l, 122r, 126r,
　　　　　　　　130r, 134r, 138, 141, 144, 148, 152, 156, 160, 164, 168, 170, 188r, 192

Yutaka Maenami　pp. 30, 40, 50, 56, 66, 70, 78, 88, 94, 104, 114l, 118l, 122l, 126l,
　　　　　　　　130l, 134l, 188l

新宮 晋 ＋ レンゾ・ピアノ

対談：平行人生

A conversation between
Susumu Shingu and Renzo Piano

Parallel Lives

新宮 晋 ＋レンゾ･ピアノ

対談：平行人生

<table>
<tr>
<td>新宮 晋
(以下、新宮)</td>
<td>初めて会った時のことを覚えてる？　大阪のヒルトン･ホテルのロビーだった。関西国際空港の
コンペに勝って、あなたが大阪に来た時のことだった。はじめからぼくに会いたいというので、
びっくりしたんだけれど。</td>
</tr>
<tr>
<td>レンゾ･
ピアノ
(以下、ピアノ)</td>
<td>そうだった。最初はホテルで次に山奥のアトリエで会ったね。ホテルで会った時、ピーター･ライス
（1935-92年）※1 も一緒にいた。</td>
</tr>
<tr>
<td>新　宮</td>
<td>うん、いたね。初めて会った時、あなたはぼくがイタリア語を話すとは知らなかった。</td>
</tr>
<tr>
<td>ピアノ</td>
<td>そう、予想もしていなかった。</td>
</tr>
<tr>
<td>新　宮</td>
<td>その日は全員が日本語で話す会議が続いていたから、くたくただっただろう。夜はぼくとイタリア語
で話した。そこでぼくたちが同い年だと分かったんだ。コロンブス新大陸発見500年記念万博の
プロジェクト（p.28-37）を始める前、ぼくたちが52歳のころだ。今やそれがお互い80代になった。</td>
</tr>
<tr>
<td>ピアノ</td>
<td>時がたつのは速く、信じられない。時間はゆっくりと過ぎるが、過ぎた後はパッと消えてしまって
覚えてもいない。不思議なものだ。でも君と三田にある原っぱ（中央公園）に行った日のことを
覚えている。例のジェノヴァ博のモデル（模型、p.12）をもってきてくれたね。</td>
</tr>
</table>

ジェノヴァ港再開発+《コロンブスの風》　Re-development of the Genoa Old Harbour + *Columbus's Wind*

A conversation between Susumu Shingu and Renzo Piano

Parallel Lives

Susumu Shingu ("Shingu")	Do you remember the first time we met? It was the lobby of the Hilton Hotel in Osaka. You had won the competition for Kansai International Airport, and it was the time you came to Osaka. Right from the start, you had apparently said you wanted to meet me, so I was surprised.
Renzo Piano ("Piano")	That's right. We met first at the hotel and then at your atelier deep in the mountains. When we met at the hotel, Peter Rice (1935-92)[*1] was with me too.
Shingu	Yes, I remember. When we first met, you didn't know I spoke Italian.
Piano	Right, I hadn't even imagined you could.
Shingu	That day, you had to attend a string of meetings all in Japanese, and looked dead beat, but that evening, you got to speak Italian with me. That's when we found out we were the same age. That was before the start of the Columbus Quincentenary project (p.28-37), so we must have been fifty-two. Now we're both in our 80s.
Piano	It's unbelievable how time flies. Well, actually, it passes slowly, but once it's gone, it just disappears and I forget everything. It's strange. But I remember the day when we went to that park in Sanda (Central Park). You brought the model for the Genoa Expo (p.12).

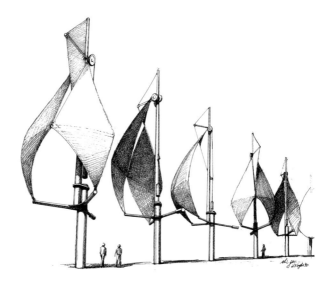

新宮晋《コロンブスの風》デッサン　Susumu Shingu, *Columbus's Wind*, drawing

011

新　宮　　その時のことはよく覚えてるよ。持参したモデルの帆を動かそうとしたけど、上手くいかず「ダメだ、できない」となった。そこで、ピーターに「実現する可能性はある？」と尋ねたら、「全ては可能だ」と言ってくれた。実際には、作品の近くに昼も夜もずっと操作する船員が要るという問題はあったけど、そのときの彼の言葉はとても印象に残っている。あれから29年経ち、お互いにこんな年になるとは考えていなかった。少年だった頃もあったのに。

[左] 三田中央公園にて（1990年）　[中央]《コロンブスの風》のプロトタイプ（1989-90年）　[右]《コロンブスの風》（1992年）
Left : in Sanda city "Chuo" park (1990)　*Center* : Prototypes for *Columbus's Wind*(1989-90)　*Right* : *Columbus's Wind*(1992)

ピアノ　　本当にそうだね。でも、まだ少年だ。「若者になるには時間が必要だ」と言った人がいる。たくさん時間をかけたから、今まさに……

新　宮　　ようやく私たちも子どもに近づいてきた（笑）。

ピアノ　　子どもにね（笑）。青年期の記憶や自分の根っこに関わることというのは、若いうちは気にならないものだし、幸いにも考えない。根っこについて考えるのは、自分の内面を観察する作業でもあるから、そこに縛られてしまうと動けなくなってしまう。必要な時点で考えればいいんだ。年を取り60歳前後から70歳くらいになると、もはや自分は自分だ。さらに70歳を過ぎるとその重要性を理解し始める。この年で生きていけるのは、何をしたかではなく何をするか。これからのことで生かされる。

新　宮　　そのとおり。思えばぼくたちはたくさんのことをしてきたね。一緒に取り組んだプロジェクトは10件あった。実現しなかったこともあるし、実はそっちのほうが興味深く思うこともたくさんあるよ。でも、ぼくたちにはこれからまだやるべきことがある。創造を続けるために、ぼくは「地球アトリエ」※2を計画しているし、あなたは財団※3をつくった。

ピアノ　　そう、君の地球アトリエと同じような経緯でつくった。それにぼくの財団は日本で生まれたんだよ。アイデアが浮かんだのは、妻のミッリや安藤忠雄と一緒に、伊勢神宮に行った時だ。2日かけて木材を保管しておく場所や作業場などいろいろ見てまわった。伊勢神宮は2つある社殿のうち、20年ごとに片方を新しくする。それが人生の暗喩だと気付いたんだ。まず20歳の時に「来なさい」そして「習いなさい」。社殿の建設を学ぶには20年かかるから、きちんと学ぶための期間だ。そして40歳で造れるようになるから「社殿を造りなさい」。さらに60歳になると「造り方を教えなさい」

Shingu   Yes, I remember that well. I tried to get the sails of the model I'd brought to move, but it didn't work, and I was like, "Sorry, it's no good." So I asked Peter, "Do you think it's going to be feasible?" and he replied "Anything is possible." It later turned out that the work would need a sailor nearby to operate it night and day, but Peter's response left a deep impression on me. Some twenty-nine years have gone by since then. We were just kids — boys. It never occurred to me at that time that we'd become so old.

Piano   Yeah, right. But we're still boys. Someone once said, "it takes a long time to become young." Well, we've had some long innings, so…

Shingu   Hah, so we're finally approaching childhood!

Piano   Childhood, yes. When we're young, things like memories of adolescence and what sits at our core don't bother us, so thankfully, we don't think about them. Thinking about our essence involves introspection, and if we do too much of that, it constrains us and prevents us from going where we want. It's something you should do only when you need to. When you put on years and get into your sixties and seventies, you're finally yourself, what you were destined to be. And from around the age of seventy, you begin to appreciate how important this is. When you get to be this age, what counts is what you do with your life, not what you've done. It's what you do that keeps you alive.

Shingu   I agree. When you think about it, we've done a lot. We've worked on ten projects together. There were others that didn't happen in the end, including many that I think were even more interesting than those that did come to fruition. But we still have work to do. I'm planning my Atelier Earth[*2], and you've created a foundation.[*3]

Piano   Yes, I created my foundation for the same kind of reasons as your Atelier Earth. By the way, did you know my foundation was conceived in Japan? The idea came to me when I went to the Ise Grand Shrine with my wife Milly, together with Tadao Ando. We spent two days visiting the locations where the timbers are stored and the workshops and so on.
The Ise Grand Shrine has two shrines, one of which is rebuilt every twenty years. This struck me as being a metaphor for life. Firstly, the age of twenty stands for "come and learn." It takes twenty years to develop the skills to build a shrine like that, so the next twenty years are for learning those skills properly. The age of forty, by which time you'll have learned enough, stands for "build the shrine," and the age of sixty, for "teach others those skills." The concept of rebuilding the shrine, effectively ensuring it remains for eternity, is based on the repetition of a cycle of processes, namely learn, create, teach. In my mind, that cycle describes life.

Shingu   It's very different from Western thinking, isn't it?

Piano   Yes, it's even more long-lived than stone. It's very Japanese, or rather, oriental in nature. I was sixty at the time, and I remember thinking that maybe it was time for me to start giving something back. And that's how the idea of the foundation was born over twenty years ago.

となる。社殿を造り直すという発想、つまり永遠あるいは恒久的な長命が、行為の反復によって成り立つことになる。学び、造り、そして教えるという行為を繰り返して継続させるという発想。これは人生の表現だ。

新　宮　こうしたやり方は西洋の考え方とはだいぶ違う。

ピアノ　石の寿命より長く、非常に日本らしいというか、東洋の発想だ。その時、ぼくは60歳だったから、何かを還元し始めるべき年齢なのかと考えた。財団のアイデアはこうして20年以上前に生まれたんだ。それで少しずつ準備をしてお金を集めた。といっても、大きな献金は受けていないから事務所のお金しかないけれど。財団のいいところは若者たちがいることだ。その中で過ごしながら、何よりもまず若者に与える。

新　宮　与えるけれど、若者から得るものも多い。喜び、好奇心、感動、そういうものが継続的にある。

ピアノ　若者の純粋さや軽快な感じ、幸福感、期待感……彼らから受け取るものは無限にある。それに若者といる時は、うそをついてはいけないし、バカなことは言えない。純粋なまなざしを前にして、率直でなくてはならない。本当の自分でいるしかないし、偽るのはみっともないしね。与える、そして得るという関係性の中に真実を語る環境をつくることができるから、年を取ったら近くに若者がいるといい。それに彼らは前を向いているから未来について話すだろう？　ずっと前に進み続ける。なんだか元気が出るんだ。若者とテーブルを囲んで議論して仕事をするとき、彼らがいいアイデアを出してくると、自分が思いつくよりうれしいものだ。人が勇気を出した場面に遭遇する、そういう喜びがある。いいアイデアを思いつくためには、アイデアを出すと決意する必要があるんだ。本気になる、飛び込む、バカなことを言う勇気を出す。

新　宮　余計な心配はせず、勇気を出す。そのことで逆に勇気を与えるんだね。

ピアノ　そう。誰にでも、文章でも絵でも工作でも、何かできた物を見て「ぼくが作った」と感動した経験はあるだろう。ぼくは16歳の時だった。何を作ったかはよく覚えてないけど、ぼくが作ったものを見て、10歳年上の兄が「えっ！　うまい、すごいな！」と驚いてくれたんだ。予想外のことだった。これが未来をつくるんだ。若者にそういうことを教えたい。マルグリット・ユルスナール（1903-87年）というフランス人の偉大な作家がいて「アイデアは闇を見る勇気がある時に浮かぶ」と言っていた。闇は少し待つと目が慣れて見えてくる。アイデアも同じで、最初は何も見えないし、あるのは雑然としたイメージだけだ。でもすぐに何かを見つけようと焦らず、忍耐があれば、少しずつ見えるようになる。闇に入るには勇気が要るし、闇をしっかり見ないといけないから簡単じゃない。でもアイデアは得ようとした時にやって来るんだ。

新　宮　大切な話だ。しばしば思うことだけど、ぼくたちは友情を持ち続けてきたよね。ぼくは最近になって

I started making preparations little by little, and doing some fundraising. Mind you, we haven't had any big donations, so almost all the money comes from the office. The great thing about the foundation is the presence of young folk. So I like to spend time there, and give what I can to them.

Shingu   You give, but you also gain a lot from the young people, right? I'm sure the foundation hums continuously with joy, curiosity, and excitement.

Piano   You're right, I get so much from their genuineness and humor, their cheerfulness and hopes. And when you're with young people, you can't lie or say stupid things. In the face of their trusting gaze, you can't help but be totally frank. You have to be who you really are. You can't pretend to be someone else. When you get older, surrounding yourself with young people is a great idea, because the give and take relationship creates the perfect environment for telling the truth. And because they're always looking ahead and talking about the future, they're moving forward all the time. I find that very energizing.

When we sit around a table to work and discuss things, and they come up with a great idea, I'm happier than if I'd thought of it. That's the kind of joy you feel when you come across people being brave. To come up with a good idea, you need to commit to getting it out. You need to get serious, dive in, and have the courage to say stupid things.

レンゾ・ピアノとRPBW（ジェノヴァ）のメンバー   Renzo Piano and RPBW (Genoa) members

Shingu   Yes, don't fret over details, just be brave. And doing so girds others to be brave too.

Piano   Right. I think most people have the experience of seeing something that they've created—a poem or painting or some kind of handicraft—and feeling proud of their creation. The first time I felt that way was when I was sixteen. I don't really remember what I made, but when my brother, who was ten years older than me, saw it, he said, "Wow, that's amazing!" I was dumbstruck. That kind of moment makes the future. I want to teach young people that kind of thing.

The great French author Marguerite Yourcenar (1903-87) once talked about having "the courage to look into the darkness." If you wait a little while, your eyes get used to the dark, and

気付いたんだけど、自分がやろうとしているのは、実現不可能なイメージを具現化するということだ。大抵のことは、自分でするか、人に頼むかしてできるけど、実現できると分かっていることに大した価値はない。でも実現できないだろうことをイメージして、実現するのがぼくの仕事だと思う。できないことだけを考えたいんだよ。あなたと仕事をしているとアイデアが湧いてくる。自分が思いつくとは予想もしなかったようなことを引き出されている。

ピアノ　それはぼくたちに親和性があるからだ。イタリア語で「選択的親和性」というんだけど、人間の過去の類似性のことをあらわしている。君は日本、ぼくはイタリアでそれぞれ違う人生を歩んできたけど、自分を駆り立てるもの、熱望や好奇心、人間性に関わる部分が似ていて、それが創造性でもある。君は芸術家で建築家、ぼくは建築家。科学者も、音楽家も、映画を作る人も、違う人生を歩みながらも親和性を抱く相手がきっといるだろう。アメリカではこの神秘をケミストリーと言う。ただ「化学」だと味気ないし、単なる化学反応ではなく人が歩んできた人生と関係がある。ぼくたちの「平行人生」（カバー絵を参照）のように収束が生じて、ある時点でトン！と互いの経験が交差する。そこに友情が生まれる。友情は共に過ごした年数で決まるものではなく親和性がどれだけ強かったかで決まる。

新　宮　そうだね。

ピアノ　例えば君は、常に軽さを追求してきた。君の理由でね。ぼくも常に重さよりも軽さを重視した。父親（カルロ・ピアノ）がセメントやレンガでできた従来型の重たく素朴な建物を造っていたから、真逆のことをしたかったのかもしれない。あるいは海の近くに生まれたせいかもしれない。ジェノヴァ港に行くと船は浮いていて地面に固定された物ではないし、空にはクレーンが漂っていて浮遊感があるからね。理由はひとつではないと思う。でもこの軽さがぼくの固定観念で、余分をそぎ落して本質に導くものだ。君の作品も同じように、空気や風、水で動くとか、軽さや不安定さがある。大ざっぱにいうと、君が創る軽さもぼくが創る軽さも重力に対する挑戦だよね。君の場合は物を動かして、バランスをとりながらずっと重力に対抗してきた。重力は自然の法則だから、とても堅固で永久不変だし勝ち目がないけど、それはぼくにも共通する。

レンゾ・ピアノ「イル・ソーレ24オーレ本社」+新宮晋《光の雲》
Renzo Piano's "Il Sole 24 Ore" Headquarters + Susumu Shingu's *Cloud of Light*

you're able to make things out. The same goes for ideas. At first, you can't see anything, and all you have is some jumbled notion. But if you're patient and don't try to find something right away, things slowly come into view. It takes courage to enter the darkness, and it's not easy either, because you have to scrutinize it carefully. But ideas come when you try looking for them.

Shingu   This is an important theme. Perhaps it's related to something else I often think about: how we've continued to be friends all these years. It was only recently that I realized I'm trying to give shape to something that can't really be done. I can do most things myself or get others to do them, but there's little value in things you know you can do. I see my job as to dream up things that can't be done and make them happen. I just want to think about stuff that can't be done. When I'm working with you, ideas come easily. I find myself dreaming up stuff that I never imagined I would come up with.

Piano   That's because of the affinity we share. In Italian, we call this *l'affinità elettiva* (elective affinity), which refers to similarities in people's pasts. You and I have lived different lives respectively in Japan and Italy, but where our interests, aspirations, curiosity and humanity is concerned, we share a lot of similarities, and creativity is also a big part of that. You're an artist and architect, and I'm an architect. I'm sure that the same goes for scientists, musicians, and filmmakers too. They probably all feel a strong affinity with certain others despite leading different lives. Americans like to call this mysterious thing "chemistry," but chemistry is too bland an expression, for one thing, and we're talking here about the lives people have led rather than just a chemical reaction. Like our "parallel lives" (as expressed in the cover art), you get this convergence until, suddenly at some point in time, experiences collide, and bang!—friendship is born. Friendship isn't about the number of years you spend together, but rather about the strength of your affinity.

Shingu   I agree.

Piano   You, for example, are constantly pursuing lightness. You have your own reasons, but I too have always put priority on lightness rather than heaviness. Maybe it's because my father (Carlo Piano) built simple, heavy buildings the old way with bricks and mortar that I wanted to do the exact opposite, or maybe it's because I was born near the sea. If you go to the port of Genoa, the ships are all floating in water, unattached to the ground, and there are cranes moving around in the sky, giving a feeling of lightness. There's probably no single reason, but I'm obsessed with lightness, with stripping away anything that's not essential to get to the essence. Your work is similarly light, mercurial, moving with air, wind, and water. You could frame the lightness that you create, and the lightness I try to create as challenges to gravity. Your works are characterized by movement and balance in constant combat with gravity. Gravity is a law of nature, so it's very stable, immutable, and indefatigable. And I face the same challenge.

新　宮　　そう。常に自然と向き合ってきた。空気、風、光、軽さはぼくたちの共通点だね。でもぼくがローマ
　　　　　で勉強した影響もあると思わない？　日本の大学を卒業して23歳から29歳までの6年間を
　　　　　ローマで過ごした。もともと絵を描いていたけど、イタリアにいる6年の間に具象から抽象へ、
　　　　　そして立体、最終的には動く彫刻になった。ルネサンス芸術にも常に触れていたし、この変遷には
　　　　　環境の影響があったと思う。

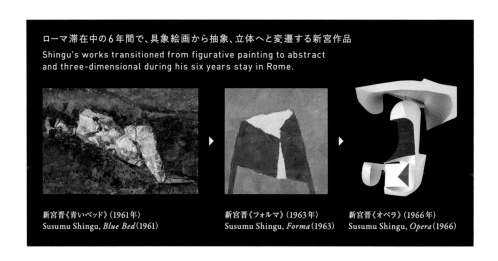

ローマ滞在中の6年間で、具象絵画から抽象、立体へと変遷する新宮作品
Shingu's works transitioned from figurative painting to abstract
and three-dimensional during his six years stay in Rome.

新宮晋《青いベッド》(1961年)　　　新宮晋《フォルマ》(1963年)　　　新宮晋《オペラ》(1966年)
Susumu Shingu, *Blue Bed*(1961)　　Susumu Shingu, *Forma*(1963)　　Susumu Shingu, *Opera*(1966)

ピアノ　　君がイタリアとルネサンスから学んで何かを得たというのは間違いないと思うけど、それは副産物
　　　　　で、親和性のほうがずっと人間の本質に関わるものだと思うよ。それでいうと、ぼくは生っ粋の
　　　　　イタリア人だけど、建築家として成長してきたなかで、常に2つの世界、日本とアメリカに惹かれて
　　　　　いた。なぜ日本かというと、光や素材が揺れる感覚に惹かれていた。織物や布地のテクスチャー
　　　　　にかかわらず、素材の質感や感触、線の交わりや明るさ、透けて見える揺らめく光とか。そこに
　　　　　自然を切り取る、あるいははめこむ能力をずっと見てきた。木を組んでひとつのまとまりにしたり、
　　　　　自然を自分のものにする感覚に接するなら日本だと。さっきの伊勢神宮の話でも、建て直し続けて
　　　　　終わりがないという考え方に惹かれ続けてきた。

新　宮　　アメリカには何年いたの？

ピアノ　　ほんの数年。アメリカの魅力は考え方。自由の感覚がある。だってイタリアに生まれたら囚人
　　　　　同然だ。美に縛られ、豊かさに縛られる。日本もそうだ。類いまれな歴史のある国だからそれに
　　　　　とらわれる危険がある。アメリカは自由と荒野の国でしがらみがなく、過去の記憶がないという
　　　　　自由がある。これは文学、演劇、舞踊、音楽についてもいえるし、詩もそうで、芸術も同じだから
　　　　　ね。自由になるには歴史を少し忘れないとダメで、意識に歴史があり過ぎると、縛られて何も
　　　　　できなくなる。

新　宮　　とはいえ、もし若い頃ローマに行かずずっと日本にいたら、さっき言った大きな変遷はなかったと思うよ。

Shingu   Right. The forces of nature have always been an integral part of our work. We both deal with air, wind, light, and lightness. But don't you think I've also been influenced by my studies in Rome? After graduating from university in Japan, I spent six years in Rome from the age of twenty-three. Painting was my thing when I started, but during my six years in Italy, I went from figurative to abstract, then three-dimensional, before finally focusing on moving sculpture. I was constantly surrounded by Renaissance art, and I think my transition was influenced by that milieu.

Piano   I'm sure that something rubbed off on you from your years in Italy and your study of Renaissance art, but I think that's only a by-product. The affinity we have has much more to do with human nature. In this respect, I'm a true-born Italian, but as I developed as an architect, Japan and America constantly fascinated me. The reason I was attracted to Japan was that sense you get of shimmering materials and light—the feel and texture of the materials regardless of what a fabric is made of, the brightness of lines and the way they intersect, the transparency of shimmering light filtering through gossamer materials. I've long been impressed by this power of Japanese aesthetics to take snippets of nature and embed it elsewhere. I've always looked to Japan to gain a sense of how to combine timbers into structures or make nature a part of whatever I'm doing. I've always been fascinated also by the idea of endlessly rebuilding as I mentioned earlier in connection with Ise Grand Shrine.

Shingu   How long were you in America?

Piano   Just a few years. I like the American way of thinking, the sense of freedom. If you grow up in Italy, after all, it's like being held hostage. You're bound by its beauty and opulence. The same goes for Japan. In countries with amazing histories, there is a danger of getting entangled in those histories. America is a land of freedom and wilderness, unfettered by memories of the past. This is true also of literature, theater, dance, music, poetry, and art. Setting yourself free requires forgetting history for a

ピアノ　　それはそうだ。それこそが人生ともいえる。もしも彼女に会わなかったらとか……。でもすべて「もしも」だから分からない。

新　宮　　なるほど。別の人生と比較はできない。

ピアノ　　知り合いだったメキシコ人のオクタビオ・パス（1914-98年）という詩人がこんなことを言っていた。「詩は偶然の所産。だが計算の結実」。だから過去のことで「もしも」と言っても、その計算は君のものだ。君はたとえローマに来なかったとしても、君の仕事をしただろう。だからあれこれ言うのは難しい。人生自体が偶然の所産であり、同時に計算の結実でもある。人は何かをし続けて偶然とのバランスをとり続ける。人生の神秘のひとつであり、人間的なあらゆる活動における真実だ。

新　宮　　すばらしい。ところで私たちは未来に何を残せるだろう。

ピアノ　　すごい質問だな。感動かな。なぜなら最終的に、芸術家は感動させるものを残す。不思議なことに、芸術品はそれを見る人に、そして生きている人の中に感動を創出する。芸術が面白いのは、ちょっとした混乱をつくるというか、驚きを創造する人の意識の中を探りに行くんだ。芸術は魂の中にある目に見えないもののベールを剥がす。内側のものを目覚めさせる。
　　　　　ぼく自身のことでいえば、財団はあるけど、真の遺産は建物だ。造った建物があって、人が訪れ建物を生きる。建物はある意味市民文化の場となって、人が出会い一緒に過ごし同じ時を生きる。美に感動するだけでなく、人々が価値を共有するという社会的で人間的な感動がある。コンサートホールを造れば、音楽があり、人が共に過ごす場、集う場になる。人と共に過ごし喜びを分かち合うんだ。芸術はさらにすばらしいものだし、映画も音楽もきっと残る。空気のように軽い物だって、写真、小説、詩、もちろん彫刻も絵画もすべて。
　　　　　君は風にそよぎ続ける物を残す。ひとつの彫刻は何十億の彫刻なんだよ。なぜなら見る瞬間ごとに違う。君の作品がパリの家にあるし他にもいくつかあるけど、時々テレビを見ないで作品を眺める。動く彫刻作品を見ていると、見るたびに変化している。時間が関与する作品だから、変わり続ける。

while. If history takes up too much space in your mind, you'll be bound by it and unable to do anything.

Shingu   Even so, if I hadn't gone to Rome when I was young, I don't think I would have gone through the major transformations that I mentioned just now.

Piano   You're right, of course. That's life, after all. What if you hadn't met the love of your life?... That kind of thing. But life is all "what if," so you really can't tell.

Shingu   So it's impossible to compare lives, right?

Piano   The Mexican poet Octavio Paz (1914-98), who was a friend of mine, described poetry as "result of chance; fruit of calculation." So even if you say "what if" about the past, it was you who took the decisions. Even if you hadn't gone to Rome, you would have gone on to do what you were destined to do. So, you really can't say. Life itself is simultaneously the product of chance and the fruit of deliberation. People keep doing stuff, balancing it with chance as they go. That's one of the mysteries of life, and true to all human activities.

Shingu   That's great. But what do you think we can leave for posterity?

Piano   Wow, that's quite a question. Emotion, maybe? In the end, I think artists want to leave behind something that stirs emotions. Wondrously, art can move those who view it, and in fact all people. The interesting thing about art is that it disorientates people a little, or rather, insinuates itself into people's minds, creating surprises. Art strips away the veil that hides what's in our souls. It stirs up the inner mind.
           In my own case, I have a foundation, but my real legacy is the buildings. People visit them, and experience them. Buildings become, in a sense, places of civic culture, places where people meet and spend time together. They can inspire people not only through their aesthetics, but also through the social and personal function they serve as places for people to share values. If you build a concert hall, it becomes a place where people gather to enjoy music together, to spend time with each other and share the joy.
           The arts are even more wonderful than architecture, and movies and music will surely remain. Sculptures and paintings too, and even things as light as air, such as photographs, novels, and poems. You will leave things that continue to dance in the wind. Each of those sculptures is actually billions of sculptures, since it differs each and every time it's looked at. I have your works in my house in Paris and elsewhere, and sometimes I just sit and stare at them rather than watching TV. Moving sculptures look different every time you look at them. Time has a hand in them, so they keep changing. And that's what you're leaving for posterity, works that stir emotions.

Shingu   I sometimes look at my works and wonder who made them. I find it hard to believe I made them all.

Piano   Hah, that's because you're a boy who makes something that comes as a surprise. It

何を残すかって、君はそれを残すんだよ。人を感動させる物をね。

新　宮　　自分の彫刻を見て「誰が作ったのか」と思うことがある。自分が全部作ったとは思えなくてね。

ピアノ　　君は自分で作って驚く子どもだからね（笑）。ぼくも建物を見て「本当にぼくが造った？」と思う時があるよ。

新　宮　　芸術家と建築家では違わない？　建築家がそう言っては危険では？

ピアノ　　いやいや、驚きの感覚があるのはいいことだよ。そうでないとむしろ傲慢だ。例えばポンピドー・センターはなぜこんなことができたか疑問に思うほどだ。よく造らせてくれたと思うよ。先週ニューヨークのホイットニー美術館のレストランに行ったら、そこに大勢の人が出入りしていて、街と芸術が日常的に混在する場所になっていた。ぼくはそこにいて、友人と昼食を食べたんだけど、子どもみたいに不思議な気分になったよ。

新　宮　　自分で作ったものを眺めると、たしかにある種の満足感があるね。

ピアノ　　センチメンタリズムに陥らない程度のね。物作りの職人も芸術家も、自分が作った物を満足感をもって眺めるのは当然だ。土曜日は仕事を休んで、1週間にした仕事を満足感とともに眺める。そこに謙虚さがある。満足感は決して驕りに変化してはならないし、ノスタルジーもよくないね。未来を見る妨げになるし、時には深刻な病でもある。芸術家という言葉には大きな修飾があって、崇高かつ霊的なものだとか、技術とは無縁のものだとか大仰なイメージがあるよね。でもぼくらは芸術と技術は一体だと知っている。

新　宮　　そう、まさにそこに可能性があって、研究や発明をすべきことがたくさんある。だから切り離すのは違うと思う。

ピアノ　　大抵の学術界の文化においては、芸術は技術だというと異端視されてしまう。だが、あらゆる芸術家、例えばピアニストは弦の張力に携わるし、君のようにバランスと重力に関わって物を作る芸術家だっている。振付師や舞踊家は身体に携わり、動きの調和、美しさを追求する。歌手は声の振動に携わる。全部の芸術と技術は結び付き、互いに強化し新しいものが生まれる。あらゆる詩的活動は、「偶然の所産であり計算の結実」。常にこの2つがともに作用する。ところが残念ながら世間の文化は、技術と芸術を別の世界に分けている。芸術は崇高で哲学的で霊的なもの、技術は手段であり重要性の低いもの。そうして飾りや権威に陥ってしまう。

新　宮　　2つのバランスを保つことが重要だ。一方が過ぎると技術ばかりが取り沙汰される。

happens to me too. I'll look up at a building and think, "Did I really build that?"

Shingu   You don't think there's any difference between artists and architects? Isn't it dangerous for an architect to say something like that?

Piano   Not at all, I think a sense of surprise is a good thing. Otherwise it's rather arrogant. Take the Pompidou Center, for example. I sometimes wonder how I managed to make something like that. They were very brave to let me. And I still get surprised by the Whitney Museum of American Art in New York. I went for a meal at the restaurant last week, and the museum was packed with people coming and going. It's a place where the city and art cross paths on a daily basis. I was there having lunch with a friend, and the whole atmosphere was so magical that I was just like a boy, drinking it in.

［左］レンゾ・ピアノ「ポンピドー・センター」（フランス、パリ）（1981年）　［右］レンゾ・ピアノ「ホイットニー美術館」（アメリカ、ニューヨーク）（2014年）
Left : Renzo Piano's Centre Georges Pompidou (Paris, France) (1981)
Right : Renzo Piano's The Whitney Museum of American Art (New York, USA) (2014)

Shingu   I must admit it that I too get a certain satisfaction from looking at the works I've made.

Piano   And that's not being sentimental, is it? I think it's only natural for craftsmen and artists to look at their works with a sense of satisfaction. On Saturdays, I take a break from work and look at the work I've done during the week, and feel satisfaction when I do so. There's humility in this. Satisfaction should never turn into arrogance, and nostalgia should also be avoided, since it gets in the way when we should be looking to the future. It can even become a serious ailment. The word "artist" has a lot of connotations, and tends to conjure up an exaggerated image of grandeur and spirituality, and having nothing to do with technology, but we know that art and technology go hand-in-hand, don't we?

Shingu   Absolutely, that's what opens the way to new possibilities. We still need to do a lot of research and invention, and technology is an integral part that shouldn't be treated separately.

Piano   In most academic circles, you're seen as a heretic if you mention technology in the same breath as art. But all artists engage with technology. Pianists, for example,

ピアノ　　行きつ戻りつの繰り返しで変化するんだよ。例えば、朝10時、君は霊的な芸術家。10時15分、建築家になる。10時30分に芸術家に戻り、11時にまた建築家になる。こうした循環がなければ芸術は権威となり形式となる。

新　宮　　きっとそれがあなたの神髄なんだね。常に新しいものを創造し実現し続けている。どこにそんなエネルギーが？

ピアノ　　偶然だよ。建築家は毎回全く異なるテーマを前にする。ある時はアメリカで美術館を造り、次はアフリカで病院を造る。毎回、バカになる必要がある。唯一そこに持ち込めるのは自分の描き方、エッセンスだけだ。スタイルではなく、欲求や熱望、生き方というような一貫性のある基準だ。それ以外は全部違うことをするんだ。

録画：Mitsuharu Tanida（SPOON Co., Ltd.）（「Parallel Lives 平行人生」展会場で上映のビデオは本対談の一部）
※2018年3月7日にRPBWパリ事務所で行われた対談を加筆修正のうえ掲載
イタリア語書き起こし・伊日翻訳・映像編集：イタリア文化会館-大阪

※注1［ピーター・ライス］
構造エンジニア。ポンピドー・センターの設計でオーヴ・アラップ社のチーフ・デザイン・エンジニアを務める。1976-80年、レンゾ・ピアノと石田俊二、岡部憲明とともにPIANO RICE ASSOCIATESを設立。1981年、R. F. R.事務所を設立。1992年に逝去するまでレンゾ・ピアノと協働した。

※注2［地球アトリエ］
兵庫県三田市の県立有馬富士公園内にある「新宮晋 風のミュージアム」に隣接して「サンダリーノの里」（子ども広場）が建設される。新宮が創り出した宇宙人「サンダリーノ」と地球の子どもたちが仲良く学ぶ地球の未来とアートの世界。風で動く巨大サンダリーノのシンボル・モニュメントが立ち、子どもたちの落書き壁が立ち並ぶ施設。

※注3［レンゾ・ピアノ財団］
イタリアで次世代を教育する場として設立された。日本を含め世界各国から若手建築家を受け入れ、後進の育成にも力を入れている。

（左から）新宮晋、フィリップ・グウベ（RPBW代表）、レンゾ・ピアノ
RPBWパリ事務所には、新宮が制作した《White Shadow》が飾られている。この作品は、2015年11月13日に28歳でパリで起こったテロの犠牲となった、元RPBW所員のドイツ人建築家ラファエル・ヒルツを追悼するものとして依頼を受け、制作された。彼を偲んで作品を見上げる3人。

From left : Susumu Shingu, Philippe Goubet (representative of RPBW), Renzo Piano Shingu's *White Shadow* is suspended in RPBW's Paris office. It was commissioned in memory of German architect Raphael Hilz who was employed by RPBW, but lost his life in Paris to the terrorist attack on November 13, 2015. Shingu, Goubet, and Piano take a moment to remember Hilz.

leverage the tension of strings, and artists like you play with balance and gravity to create works. Choreographers and dancers engage with the body to seek harmony and beauty of movement. Singers make use of vocal vibrations. All arts and technologies are connected, with new stuff emerging from the way the reinforce each other. All poetic activity is the result of chance and the fruit of calculation. The two always work together. Unfortunately, though, everyday perspectives on culture are always trying to separate technology and art from each other. Art is seen as sublime, philosophical, and spiritual, while technology is belittled as just a means to an end. From there, culture goes downhill, becoming a means of ornament or following the dictates of cultural authorities.

Shingu   You need to strike a balance between the two. If you go too far in the other direction, technology hogs the limelight.

Piano   Change happens by repeatedly going back and forth between the two. For example, you might be a spiritual artist at 10 a.m., and then turn into an architect at 10:15. At 10:30, you're back in artist mode, and at 11, you've become an architect again. Without this kind of cycle, art degrades into formality and authority.

Shingu   That change is no doubt what's at your core. You're always experimenting and creating new stuff. Where do you find that energy?

Piano   It's just coincidence. Architects face completely different challenges with each new project. You might be working on an art museum in America one month, and on a hospital in Africa the next month. You have to void your mind each time. And the only thing that enables you to do so is your essence, the way you see yourself. It's not about style, but rather about constants such as your desires, aspirations, the way you live your life. Other than that, you have to do everything differently.

Recorded by Mitsuharu Tanida (SPOON Co., Ltd.)
(Parts of this conversation are featured in the video screened at the Parallel Lives exhibition venue.)
Video transcribed, translated and edited from Italian to Japanese by Italian Cultural Institute in Osaka.
*This conversation took place at RPBW's Paris Office on March 7, 2018.
It has been edited and translated into English from the Japanese version for inclusion in this publication.

Notes
1. Peter Rice: Structural engineer who served as Ove Arup & Partners' chief design engineer for the Pompidou Center project. From 1976 to 1980, he worked with Renzo Piano, Shunji Ishida, and Noriaki Okabe as Piano Rice Associates, and in 1981, founded RFR. He worked with Renzo Piano right up to his death in 1992.

2. Atelier Earth: Susumu Shingu's Atelier Earth concept includes a children's recreation area named Sandarino no Sato to be built next to the Susumu Shingu Wind Museum in Arimafuji Park in Sanda, Hyogo Prefecture. This is a venue where children will join Sandarino, an alien created by Shingu, to learn about art and the future of the earth. The project features a huge Sandarino symbol monument that moves with the wind, and walls for children to decorate with graffiti.

3. Renzo Piano Foundation (Fondazione Renzo Piano): Established in 2004 in Genoa, Italy, as a facility to educate and train future generations, the foundation opens its doors to young architects from throughout the world, including Japan.

新宮晋とレンゾ・ピアノ　RPBW（ジェノヴァ）にて　2022年　Susumu Shingu and Renzo Piano at RPBW Genoa in 2022

新宮 晋＋レンゾ·ピアノ
10のコラボレーション

Susumu Shingu + Renzo Piano
10 Collaborations

レンゾ・ピアノ Renzo Piano　　　　　新宮 晋 Susumu Shingu

ジェノヴァ港再開発 ＋ コロンブスの風
Re-development of the Genoa Old Harbour　Columbus's Wind

ジェノヴァ港再開発 Re-development of the Genoa Old Harbour

RPBWは1992年のコロンブス新大陸発見500年記念万博に際し、ジェノヴァ港と、その港に面したカリカメント広場の再開発に携わった。意図されたのは、19世紀から1960年代までに建造されたほとんど使われていない旧税関、港湾の建物や高架道路により市街地と港の間に生じた物理的、心理的分断を解消し、自然な繋がりを取り戻すことである。長期的な視点での都市再開発計画の一環としてのポルト・アンティーコ（旧港）の再生であり、ジェノヴァ一般市民に開放され、港岸エリアを楽しめるようになって現在に至っている。この際、万博のシンボルとなった「ビゴ」と既存の埠頭の上にフェスティヴァル会場、水族館が新設された。ビゴとはイタリア語でクレーン船のジブとその先端のことで、その形を模した8本の白い軸が展望エレベーターとフェスティヴァル広場のテント構造を支えている。ビゴとフェスティバル広場と一体化して、新宮晋の彫刻《コロンブスの風》が9体並んでいる。

In 1992, at the time of the *International Exhibition Genoa '92 - Colombo '92 (Columbus International Exposition)* celebrating 500 years since Columbus discovered America, RPBW took part in the redevelopment of Genoa's old harbor as well as Piazza Caricamento situated adjacent to the harbor. The aim was to remove the physical and psychological barrier created between the city and the harbor by the mostly unused old customs office and harbor buildings that had been constructed between the nineteenth century, and by an elevated road, and thereby restore the natural connection between the two areas. This revitalization of the Porto Antico (old port) was part of a long-term urban redevelopment project,and resulted in the port being opened to the general public of Genoa, allowing people to visit the port to enjoy the area along the waterside. That advantage remains today. At the time, RPBW created the Bigo, a symbol of the expo, as well as the Piazza delle Feste (festival plaza) and the aquarium on an existing pier. "Bigo" is an Italian word referring to a floating crane mechanism. Here, eight white masts modeled after a bigo support the Bigo Panoramic Lift and the tent structure of the Piazza delle Feste. The Bigo and Piazza delle Feste form one unit, with nine sculptures by Susumu Shingu called *Columbus's Wind* arrayed nearby.

PROJECT DATA	所在地	イタリア、ジェノヴァ	Location	Genoa, Italy
	デザイン・工期	1985-2001年	Design and Construction	1985-2001
	彫刻	1992年 制作	Sculpture	Produced in 1992

《コロンブスの風》（1992年） *Columbus's Wind* (1992)

不可能なものは何もない

Nothing is impossible

——— ピーター・ライス Peter Rice ※

1992年ジェノヴァ旧港で、コロンブスの新大陸発見500年記念万博が開かれた。これは老朽化したこのエリアの再開発を兼ねた大プロジェクトで、レンゾ・ピアノが既存の旧税関、港湾倉庫等を再利用して、博覧会会場に使い、後に会議場、水族館、展望エレベーター、フェスティヴァル広場として一般市民の憩いの場として開放した。新宮が依頼を受けたのは、コロンブスの帆船サンタ・マリア号をイメージしたモニュメントを提案することだった。新宮は夢中になって次々と浮かぶアイデアを試作した。その頃このプロジェクトに参加していた天才構造エンジニアのピーター・ライスと新宮は、初めて会ったときから気が合ったが、ピーターはいつも新宮の提案を楽しみにしていて適切なアドヴァイスをした。かなり奇抜なアイデアに対しても「不可能なものは何もない」と言い切った。こうして生まれた高さ19m、9体の《コロンブスの風》は現在も海風、山風を受けて元気に回り続け、人々で賑わうポルト・アンティーコの風景に溶け込んでいる。

The *International Exhibition Genoa ' 92 - Colombo ' 92 (Columbus International Exposition*) celebrating 500 years since Columbus discovered America was held in 1992. This was a major project coinciding with the redevelopment of a run-down district, and Renzo Piano re-used the existing former customs house, warehouses, and other harbor buildings as exposition venues. After the exposition finished, they were opened as public amenities comprising a conference hall, an aquarium, a panoramic elevator, and the Piazza delle Feste (festival plaza).Shingu was asked to devise a monument inspired by the Santa Maria, one of Columbus's sailing ships. He threw himself into the project, creating numerous prototypes based on one idea after another. Since their first meeting, Shingu had always got on well with Peter Rice, the structural engineering genius who was also involved in this project at the time, and Peter had always looked forward to Shingu's proposals and offered appropriate advice. Even for the most outrageous ideas, he would respond confidently that "Nothing is impossible." The result was *Columbus's Wind*, nine 19m-high sculptures that continue to revolve briskly in the sea breezes and mountain winds, and which have become an integral part of the scenery of the lively Porto Antico (old port).

※ ピーター・ライス（1935-92年）
構造エンジニア。ポンピドー・センターの設計でオーヴ・アラップ社のチーフ・デザイン・エンジニアを務める。1976-80年、レンゾ・ピアノと石田俊二、岡部憲明とともにPIANO RICE ASSOCIATESを設立。1981年、R.F.R.事務所を設立。1992年に逝去するまでレンゾ・ピアノと協働した。

Peter Rice (1935-92)
Structural engineer who served as Ove Arup & Partners' chief design engineer for the Pompidou Center project. From 1976 to 1980, he worked with Renzo Piano, Shunji Ishida, and Noriaki Okabe as Piano Rice Associates, and in 1981, founded RFR. He worked with Renzo Piano right up to his death in 1992.

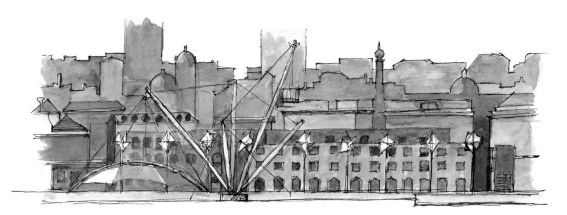

新宮晋《コロンブスの風》風景画（1992年）　Susumu Shingu, *Columbus's Wind*, landscape painting (1992)

新宮晋とレンゾ・ピアノ　ジェノヴァ港にて（1992年5月1日）
Susumu Shingu and Renzo Piano at Genoa Old Harbour (May 1, 1992)

《コロンブスの風》のプロトタイプ
Prototypes for *Columbus's Wind*

ジェノヴァ港再開発＋《コロンブスの風》　Re-development of the Genoa Old Harbour + *Columbus's Wind*

ビゴとフェスティヴァル広場＋《コロンブスの風》　The Bigo and Piazza delle Feste + *Columbus's Wind*

ビゴのジブに支えられたテント　工事完了間近の写真
Tent supported by the Bigo's jibs. Photo taken when construction neared completion.

二期目（1993-2001年）のジェノヴァ港再開発で完成した球体状の温室
Biosphere completed in Phase II (1993-2001) of the Re-development of the Genoa Old Harbour

水族館　イルカの水槽　Aquarium of Genoa, dolphins

ビゴとフェスティヴァル広場 +《コロンブスの風》 夜景
The Bigo and Piazza delle Feste + *Columbus's Wind* at night

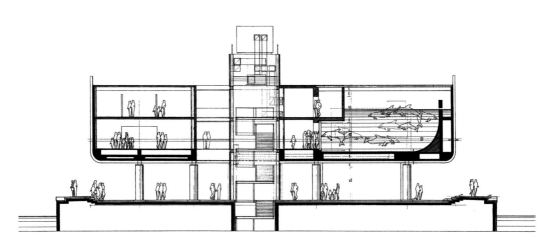

既存の埠頭の上に建てられた水族館の断面図
Aquarium of Genoa was built above of existing pier traversal section

ジェノヴァ港再開発+《コロンブスの風》 航空写真 Aerial photo of Re-development of the Genoa Old Harbour + *Columbus's Wind*

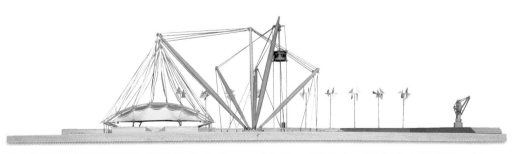

ジェノヴァ港再開発+《コロンブスの風》 模型 1:50 Re-development of the Genoa Old Harbour + *Columbus's Wind* 1:50 model

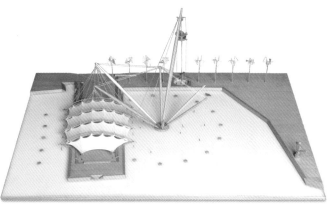

レンゾ・ピアノ Renzo Piano

関西国際空港旅客ターミナルビル ＋ はてしない空
Kansai International Airport Passenger Terminal Building

新宮 晋 Susumu Shingu

Boundless Sky

貨物ターミナルからの眺め　カーブを描いた特徴的な屋根がよく見える　From the cargo terminal, there is a good view of the passenger terminal's characteristic curved roof.

大阪湾に新設された飛行場で、1988年に実施された国内初の本格的な国際設計競技によりRPBWが設計者に決まった。人工島の建設から始め、1994年に開港。全体はグライダーが島の上に休んでいるかのような形状で、横に拡がる翼の両端幅は1.7kmにも及ぶ。波型の屋根にもかかわらず同一規格のステンレススチールパネルの開発が叶い8万2千個設置された。最上階にある国際線出発フロアの屋根は80mにも及ぶ梁がその両端で斜めの柱に支えられて、異なる半径の円から構成される波型をしている。この構造形態はフロア内の広範に及ぶ空気の拡散の流れを考慮した設計で、オーヴ・アラップ社の構造、ピーター・ライスと設備のトム・ベーカーのチームとの協働作業で発案されたものである。オープンダクトとしての天井には、間接照明として機能する反射パネルが19枚取り付けられた。ここに新宮晋の彫刻が17体ある。

RPBW became the designer for the passenger terminal of a new airport to be constructed in Osaka Bay through what was Japan's first significant international design competition, held in 1988. The airport first required construction of a man-made island, and eventually opened in 1994. The overall shape of the terminal building resembles a glider resting on the island, with the wings extending outwards on both sides, measuring 1.7km from end to end. Despite the roof's wave-like shape, RPBW managed to design it using 82,000 identical stainless steel panels. The roof of the uppermost international departures level has a wave-like shape formed of a series of arcs of different radii connected at tangent points, with beams spanning 80m following the asymmetrical form of the roof, supported at their extremities by pairs of inclined columns. The form of this structure was designed to allow the airflow to be distributed across the entire floor, and was proposed through collaboration with structural engineer Peter Rice and services engineer Tom Barker from the team at Ove Arup & Partners. The ceiling, which serves as an open-air duct, has affixed to it nineteen reflective panels that provide indirect lighting. Seventeen sculptures by Susumu Shingu are installed here.

PROJECT DATA	所在地	日本、大阪	Location	Osaka, Japan
	デザイン・工期	1988-1994年	Design and Construction	1988-1994
	彫 刻	1994年 制作	Sculpture	Produced in 1994

［上］国際線出発フロアの夜景　オープンエアダクトのパネルが見える　［下］関西国際空港旅客ターミナルビル　4F国際線出発フロア+《はてしない空》

Top : International departures floor at night, showning the open air duct panels. *Bottom* : Kansai International Airport Passenger Terminal Building 4F international departure floor + *Boundless Sky*

見えない空気の流れを見えるようにしてくれないか？

Can you make the streams of air visible?

——— レンゾ・ピアノ Renzo Piano

1989年、大阪府豊能郡の山奥にあった掘立小屋のような新宮のアトリエに、イタリアのジェノヴァから一本の電話があった。「関西空港の国際コンペで選ばれたレンゾ・ピアノが日本に行くのだが、あなたに是非会いたい」ということだった。数日後約束通り、大阪梅田のヒルトン・ホテルのロビーで、初めて二人は出会うことになった。短い英語で挨拶を交わした後、新宮がイタリア語も話せることを告げると、レンゾは「マンマミーア！（何ということだ！）」と叫んで、長年の友だちのように一気に打ち解けた。「君は世界一空気のことが分かっているアーティストだ」「私たちは美しい空気の流れをデザインすることに成功した。しかし、残念なことに誰もそれを見ることが出来ない。どうか最小限の装置で、見えるようにしてくれないか」。こんな魅力的な誘いを断る理由は何もなかった。関空の工期の関係で、ジェノヴァ港のプロジェクトの方が先に完成した。

In 1989, Shingu received a telephone call from the Italian city of Genoa in his shack-like atelier in Toyono, deep in the mountains of Osaka Prefecture. "Renzo Piano, the winner of the international competition to design Kansai International Airport, will be visiting Japan, and would like to meet you." A few days later, as promised, the two met for the first time in the lobby of the Hilton Hotel in Osaka's Umeda district. Having briefly greeted each other in English, when Shingu mentioned that he spoke Italian, Piano exclaimed *"Mamma mia!"* ("My goodness!"), and started chatting as familiarly as if they had been friends for years. "You understand the air better than any other artist in the world. We have succeeded in designing beautiful currents of air, but sadly these cannot be seen by anyone. Can you somehow make them visible, using the minimum of apparatus?" There was no reason to refuse this appealing invitation. But because construction of the artificial island on which the airport was to be built was severely delayed, he embarked on the Genoa harbor project first.

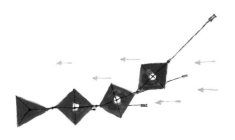

新宮晋《はてしない空》プロトタイプのスケッチ（1994年）
Susumu Shingu, *Boundless Sky* (prototype), sketch(1994)

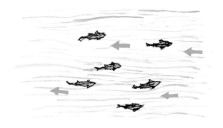

新宮晋《はてしない空》イメージスケッチ（1994年）
Susumu Shingu, *Boundless Sky*, image sketch(1994)

［左］新宮アトリエにて《はてしない空》のプロトタイプ（上）とレンゾ・ピアノ、新宮晋（左）、岡部憲明（右）（1994年）　［右］4F国際線出発フロアへ向かう渡り廊下＋《はてしない空》（右側）
Left: At Shingu Atelier. *Boundless Sky* (prototype) (above), Renzo Piano (center), Susumu Shingu (left) and Noriaki Okabe (right)
Right: 4F bridge international departure floor from the walkway entrance + *Boundless Sky* (on the right)

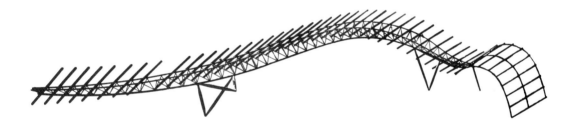

恐竜の骨組のような屋根構造体の模型「ダイナソー 2」1:50　1:50 model of the roof structure like a dinosau skelton (*Dinosaur 2*)

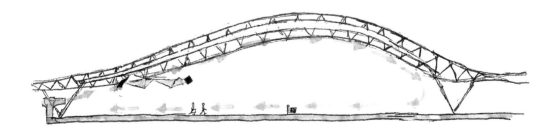

新宮晋《はてしない空》スケッチ（1994年）　Susumu Shingu, *Boundless Sky*, sketch (1994)

041

夕暮れ時の上空からの写真 竣工時（1994年）　Passenger building from the sky as the sun sets. Construction completed.(1994)

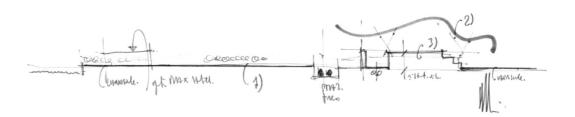

レンゾ・ピアノのスケッチ　Renzo Piano sketch

上空から空港が建てられた人工島を眺める　Airport was built on man-made Island : view from the sky

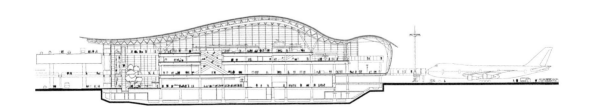

関西国際空港旅客ターミナルビル　断面図　Kansai International Airport Passenger Terminal Building cross section

関西国際空港旅客ターミナルビル　4F国際線出発フロア+《はてしない空》
Kansai International Airport Passenger Terminal Building 4F international departure floor + *Boundless Sky*

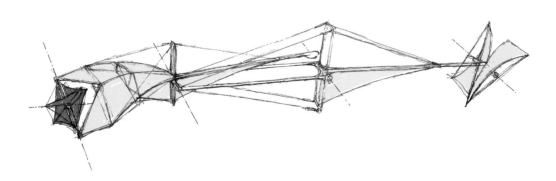

新宮晋《はてしない空》スケッチ（1994年）　Susumu Shingu, *Boundless Sky*, sketch（1994）

新宮晋《はてしない空》模型　Susumu Shingu, *Boundless Sky*, model

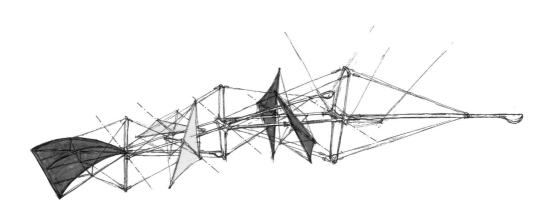

関西国際空港旅客ターミナルビル　4F国際線出発フロア+《はてしない空》
Kansai International Airport Passenger Terminal Building 4F international departure floor + *Boundless Sky*

［上］カーヴした屋根の構造体　*Top* : Curved roof structure
［右ページ］国際線ゲートラウンジ　*Right* : International gate lounge

レンゾ・ピアノ Renzo Piano　　　　　　　　　　　　　　　　　新宮 晋 Susumu Shingu

リンゴット工場再開発計画 ＋ 雨の軌跡
Lingotto Factory Conversion　　　　　　　　　　　　Locus of Rain

「リンゴット工場再開発」ジョヴァンニ＋マレッラ・アニェッリ・ピクチャー・ギャラリー　　Lingotto Factory Conversion, Giovanni and Marella Agnelli Picture Gallery

トリノにある「リンゴット・ファクトリー」は建築史上重要な近代建築であり自動車工場である。1920年代の鉄筋コンクリートによる先進的な建築で、5層立てのビルの屋上に自動車のテスト走行のためのサーキットがあることで知られる。1982年に閉鎖された後、フィアット社は設計競技を行い、RPBWが翌年勝者となってこの建築の改装に携わった。建物の外側はほとんど変更されず、内側にエキシビションセンター、会議室、ホール、ホテル、オフィス、店舗などが設計された。屋上には膨らんだ泡のようなユニークな形態をした「バブル」と呼ばれるガラスとスチール製の光あふれる会議室と絵画館が増築された。その後1997年にフィアット社マネージメント本部がこのビルに戻り、2002年にはトリノ工科大学自動車工学科もここに移転している。この敷地に新宮晋の彫刻《雨の軌跡》が設置されて来訪者たちを楽しませている。2003年、ジョヴァンニ＋マレッラ・アニェッリ・ピクチャー・ギャラリーが新たにオープンし、リンゴット工場再開発計画は完了した。

The Lingotto Factory, a car manufacturing plant in Turin, Italy, is historically significant as a prime example of modernist architecture. It was an advanced building in the 1920s, built with reinforced concrete, and famous for having a track for testing automobiles on the rooftop of the five-story building. The factory was closed in 1982, and in 1984 Fiat S.p.A. held a design competition, which RPBW won the following year, giving it the contract to convert the building. The exterior remained largely unaltered, but its interior was modified to accommodate an exhibition center, a conference center and auditorium, hotels, offices, and retail space. A uniquely shaped meeting room called "Bubble", resembling a round bubble, was added to the roof. Being made of glass and steel, it was blessed with ample light. Later, in 1997, Fiat group's management headquarters returned to the office block. In 2002, Turin Polytechnic's automotive engineering department also moved into the building. The sculpture *Locus of Rain* by Susumu Shingu installed at the site is much appreciated by visitors. The Giovanni and Marella Agnelli Picture Gallery was inaugurated in 2003, thus concluding the Lingotto building's transformation process.

PROJECT DATA	所在地	イタリア、トリノ	Location	Turin, Italy
	デザイン・工期	1983–2003年	Design and Construction	1983–2003
	彫刻	1995年制作	Sculpture	Produced in 1995

《雨の軌跡》（1995年）　*Locus of Rain*（1995）

この《雨の軌跡》にはレオナルドがいる

Trace of Leonardo in *Locus of Rain*

——— マーティン・ケンプ Martin Kemp

1923年に操業を開始した「リンゴット・ファクトリー」は、イタリアを代表する自動車メーカー、フィアット社の自動車工場である。ビルの屋上に自動車がテスト走行できるコースが備えられ、トリノの街のシンボルになっていた。大胆な発想が生かされた建物で、洒落っ気あるイタリア車の魅力の源泉が窺える。当初の役割を終えた建物は82年に閉鎖されたが、レンゾ・ピアノが手がけた再開発計画によって、往時の雰囲気を活かしつつも自然をふんだんに摂り入れた、現代的な複合施設に生まれ変わっている。1995年に設置された新宮晋の《雨の軌跡》は当初中庭にあったが外部の旧本社前に移設され、2023年3月には市長臨席のもとメンテナンスを終えて復帰の式典が行われた。《雨の軌跡》と名付けた作家のイメージする世界に、鑑賞者たちは知らずのうちに引き込まれ、我知らず穏やかで幸せなひとときを持つ。そんな時間を過ごした一人がイギリスの美術史家、マーティン・ケンプだった。レオナルド・ダヴィンチ研究の世界的第一人者である彼は、この作品を前に「この作品にはレオナルドがいる」と当時最大級の賛辞を送った。施設に設置された《雨の軌跡》は、4個のシャンペングラスのようなカップが降り注ぐ水を空中で受けて重くなり降りてくるが、こぼすと軽くなってまた昇っていく。決して繰り返すことのないランダムな回転運動は見るたびに変化をもたらす。

The Ligotto Factory, which began operation in 1923, is a car manufacturing plant owned by Fiat, one of Italy's most renowned automotive companies. A vehicle test track was constructed on the roof of the building, which had become a symbol of the city of Turin. A highly imaginative structure, it conveys something of the source of the appeal of smart Italian cars. The factory ceased production and was closed in 1982, but under the redevelopment project fronted by Renzo Piano it was reborn as a contemporary multipurpose building that incorporated abundant natural elements while making the most of its original atmosphere. Susumu Shingu's sculpture *Locus of Rain*, installed in 1995, was initially placed in the inner courtyard, but was later moved outside, in front of the former head office, and in March 2023 a ceremony in the presence of the Mayor of Turin was held to mark its return after maintenance. Viewers are unconsciously drawn into the world portrayed by the sculptor through *Locus of Rain*, instinctively enjoying a moment of quiet happiness. One visitor to have spent such moments with the sculpture is British art historian Martin Kemp. The world's foremost scholar of Leonardo da Vinci, he paid it the highest possible compliment by saying that "You can see the trace of Leonardo in this work." In *Locus of Rain*, installed inside the complex, four champagne-glass–shaped cups are filled with falling water high up in the air and descend as they grow heavier, only to become lighter and rise again when the water spills out. The work changes moment by moment as a result of random rotational movements that will never be repeated.

《雨の軌跡》(1995年)　*Locus of Rain* (1995)

上空からの撮影写真　Aerial photo

［左］リンゴット工場再開発　トリノ工科大学自動車工学科　*Left*：Turin Polytechnic's automotive engineering department inside the Lingotto Factory Conversion
［右］会議場＋コンサートホール　*Right*：Conference and Music Hall

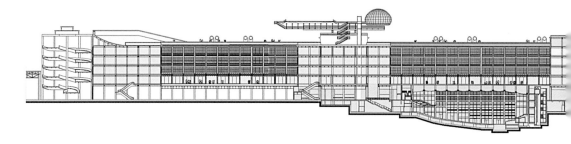

中庭　Courtyard

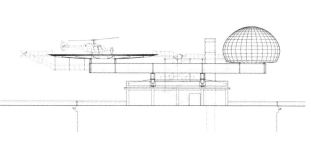

［左］会議室「バブル」　*Left* : "The Bubble" meeting room
［右］屋上に増築された「バブルとヘリポート」の断面図　*Right* : Cross section of the Bubble and heliport constracted on the roof

リンゴット工場再開発　ジョヴァンニ＋マレッラ・アニェッリ・ピクチャー・ギャラリー完成後の断面図
Lingotto Factory Conversion. Cross section after completion of Giovanni and Marella Agnelli Picture Gallery

レンゾ・ピアノ Renzo Piano
新宮 晋 Susumu Shingu

レンゾ・ピアノ・ビルディング・ワークショップ ＋ 海の響き

Renzo Piano Building Workshop Resonance of the Sea

北側からの航空写真　プンタ・ナーヴェとリグリア海　Aerial photo from the north, showing Punta Nave and the Ligurian Sea

リグリア海に面した段丘の斜面にあるRPBWのジェノヴァ本部の建物。丘の上にある事務所入口へは海と緑に囲まれながらガラスのエレベーターに乗って向かう。建築内部もこの土地と同じ段状の構造となっており、丘に沿った角度に傾斜したガラスの屋根を通して太陽光が降り注ぐよう、ルーバーを開閉するシステムが、建物内の自然光のレベルを常に最適な照度に調整する。建物の全体は、このリヴィエラ地方に典型的な温室の形状を想起させるもので、事務所内にも植栽され、緑と光と海に溢れた内と外の境界線のない環境が生み出された。建物の一番下の階からガラス越しに見える海に面した緑の斜面に、新宮晋の彫刻がある。ここは、いつも他の人々のために設計するレンゾ・ピアノが故郷ジェノヴァに自身と事務所のために考えた仕事場である。

The Genoa headquarters of the Renzo Piano Building Workshop sits perched on the slopes of the terraced coastline facing the Ligurian Sea. You head to the office entrance on the hill by taking a glass elevator, surrounded by the sea and rich vegetation. Like the surrounding landscape, the internal space of the studio steps down the hillside in a series of terraces. A glass roof sloped at the same angle as the hill lets in sunlight, with levels of natural light inside the building regulated by a system that opens and closes louvers, always maintaining the optimal level of light. The building overall brings to mind the shape of the greenhouses that are typical along the terraced Italian Riviera, and plants are grown inside the structure as well, creating an environment without boundaries between inside and outside, brimming with greenery, light, and the sea. Sculptures by Susumu Shingu situated on a green hillside facing the sea can be seen through glass from the lowest level of the building. Renzo Piano, who is always designing buildings for others, designed this architecture in his hometown Genoa to be his own studio.

PROJECT DATA	所在地	イタリア、ジェノヴァ	Location	Genoa, Italy
	デザイン・工期	1989-1991年	Design and Construction	1989-1991
	彫　刻	1995年 制作	Sculpture	Produced in 1995

《海の響き》（1995年） *Resonance of the Sea* (1995)

ウェルカム・アート
Welcome art

———— 新宮晋 Susumu Shingu

ジェノヴァの中心部から海沿いに西へ車で30分ほどのところに、斜面の段差に沿って高さをおさえて周囲の自然に同化した、光溢れるRPBWのオフィスが建っている。ガラスで覆われた小さなモノレールで傾斜地を登っていくと、その途中に《海の響き》が建っている。事務所から地中海を見下ろす位置にあり、吹き上がる風を受けて優雅に動き続ける。ここはオーダーしたピアノが毎日を過ごす日常空間でもあり、多くのスタッフが仕事をし、時に来客もある特別な場所だ。舞台は、一瞬一瞬が変化する地中海と大きな空、そこにこの彫刻が加わることで、見慣れたはずの風景にアクセントを与えている。まだこの事務所が建設中だった頃に案内されて見に来た新宮は、「いいとこだなぁ。こんなに地中海が綺麗に見えるところはそんなにないだろう」と思った。ここに彫刻があれば、それをバックにきれいな自然を感じられるのではないか、ウェルカム・アートの役割を果たすのではないかと考え《海の響き》は生まれた。今日も地中海の風に舞いながら、人々を優しく迎えていることだろう。

The light-filled RPBW offices are built on a terraced hillside around thirty minutes from central Genoa by car, with its height restricted in order to blend into the surrounding natural scenery. A small, glass-covered monorail climbs this slope, passing *Resonance of the Sea* on the way, which stands so as to look out on the Mediterranean from the offices, and continually moves gracefully in the rising breeze. This structure is both the everyday environment for Renzo Piano, who commissioned this work, the workplace for his many staff, and a special place where visitors sometimes come. The setting is the Mediterranean, which is constantly changing from moment to moment, and the expansive sky, and placing this sculpture in this context accentuates what should be a familiar landscape. Shingu was asked to provide a sculpture, and, making a visit while the offices were still under construction, thought "This is a great place. There can't be many places where the Mediterranean looks as lovely as this." *Resonance of the Sea* is born out of the idea that if there were a sculpture here, viewers would be able to feel the beautiful natural landscape in the background, and it would therefore function as "welcome art." Today, it continues to graciously welcome people as it dances in the Mediterranean wind.

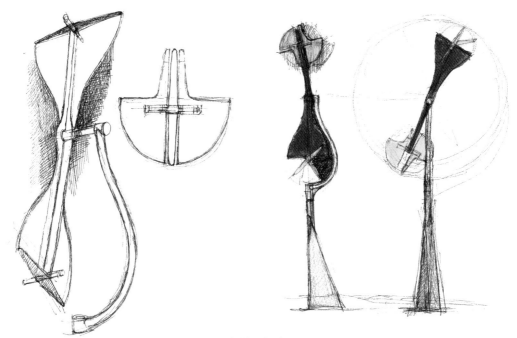

新宮晋《海の響き》スケッチ　　Susumu Shingu, *Resonance of the Sea*, sketch

［左］《海の響き》　［右］《海の響き》とレンゾ・ピアノ（左）、新宮晋・保子（中央）、石田俊二（右）（1996年）
Left : *Resonance of the Sea*　*Right* : Resonance of the Sea with Renzo Piano (left), Susumu and Yasuko Shingu (center), Shunji Ishida (right). (1996)

RPBW事務所とレンゾ・ピアノ財団を海側から撮影した写真
Renzo Piano Building Workshop and Fondazione Renzo Piano viewed from the sea

レンゾ・ピアノのスケッチ　Renzo Piano sketch

RPBWに向かうケーブルカー（北側から撮影）
Cablecar heading toward Renzo Piano Building Workshop
(photographed from the north)

俯瞰図　Bird's eye view

全体模型 1:100　Overall model 1:100

夜に撮影された上空からの写真　Aerial photograph at night

《海の響き》（1995年）　*Resonance of the Sea*（1995）

《海の響き》とリグリア海　*Resonance of the Sea* and the Ligurian Sea

透明性、光のヴァイブレーション、大気に満ちた事務所内部
Renzo Piano Building Workshop, incorporating transparency, light's vibration along with the shape and volume, and airiness

レンゾ・ピアノ Renzo Piano　　　　　　　　　　　新宮 晋 Susumu Shingu

メリディアーナ・センター ＋ 雲との対話
Meridiana Shopping Center and Offices　　　Dialogue with Clouds

《雲との対話》(1998年)　*Dialogue with Clouds*(1998)

イタリア、ロンバルディア州北部のアルプス山脈に近い町、レッコ中心部の5万3千平米の敷地にあるビル。3万2千平米の広い緑地公園に囲まれて、正方形の敷地の三層には、ハイパーマーケット（郊外にある倉庫型スーパーマーケット）や店舗が展開されている。また2千台収容可能な巨大駐車場もあり、この建築計画により都市機能の戦略的復帰がなされた。レッコは避暑地として知られるコモ湖の南東の端に位置し、山と緑、湖のある美しい景観の地。「メリディアーナ」とはイタリア語で日時計の意味で、ガラスのファサードの三棟の建築の並びを上空から俯瞰すると半円を描く。湖面のように深い水色のガラスのファサードは、光を反射し輝きながらこの地の四季折々の豊かな自然を映し出す。新宮晋の風見は5つの塔の上に立っている。

A multipurpose complex on a 53,000sqm site in the center of Lecco, a town in northern Lombardy close to the Alps. Residential and office towers look down on 32,000sqm of green parkland. Underneath, a rectangular built area on three levels contains a hypermarket and shops, with associated parking for 2,000 vehicles. The objective of the architectural design was a strategic restoration of the town's urban function. Lecco is situated at the southeastern end of the summer retreat of Lake Como, and the combination of mountains, greenery, and lake give the area a reputation for beautiful scenery. "Meridiana" is the Italian term for a sundial, and the three towers with their glass facades are arranged in a semicircle when viewed from above. The deep blue appearance of the glass facades echoes the blue of the lake, reflecting light and the natural beauty of the surroundings as they change around the year. Five sculptures by Susumu Shingu are installed at the highest points of the buildings.

PROJECT DATA	所在地	イタリア、レッコ	Location	Lecco, Italy
	デザイン・工期	1988-1999年	Design and Construction	1988-1999
	彫 刻	1998年 制作	Sculpture	Produced in 1998

［上］《雲との対話》（1998年）　［下］メリディアーナ・センター　上空から敷地全域を撮影した写真

Top: Dialogue with Clouds (1998)　　*Bottom*: Meridiana Shopping Center and Offices. Aerial view of the whole site

上を向いて歩こう
Looking up

——— 新宮晋 Susumu Shingu

「ここ（イタリア北部の町、レッコ）のショッピングセンターの屋上に風見を考えてくれないか」。RPBWの
オフィスでそう依頼されたのがはじまりだった。新宮が図面を見ると、半円形の敷地に高さ60mの塔5つ
をつなぐように建てたユニークな建物が描かれていた。全ての塔の上に巨大な風見を付け、5つの風を求めて
動き続ける巨大な風見のアイデアが浮かんだ。同時に、コモ湖湖畔の風光明媚な自然環境の中で地上を
歩く人たちがこの風見のあるショッピングセンターを眺め、いつも上を向いて歩きたくなるような、少なくとも
高さ6mぐらいの巨大な風見を作ろうと新宮は考えた。風見とは呼べないほどの大きさだ。そうなると、作り
慣れた日本の工場で作るという訳にはいかないので、作ってくれる所を探すことから始めなければならなかった。
すると骨格と外皮を、イタリアで普段は天井を製作している工場が作ってくれることになり、重要な回転部
のパーツはユーロ・ディズニーの遊具を作っている別の会社が請け負ってくれることになった。何もかも
初めてのことで、上手くいくだろうかと新宮は心配したが、作業は最後まで問題なく進んだ。上手く行くときは、
すべてがひとつの目的のために、チームとして動くからだ。無事設置された作品は、風に向かって5つの作品
がそれぞれ自由に動き、雲たちとの会話を楽しんでいるようだ。

It started with a request made at the RPBW office. "Could you think up a weathervane for the roof
of the shopping center here [the northern Italian city of Lecco] ?" When Shingu looked at the
plans, he saw that they depicted a unique building, constructed of five linked 60m-high towers
built on a semicircular site. He had the idea of topping the towers with five giant weathervanes that
would be in continual motion in search of the wind. He also thought that he would make these
giant weathervanes at least around 6m high, so that people strolling at ground level amid the scenic
landscape of Lake Como would gaze at this shopping center with its weathervanes, and want to be
constantly looking up as they walked. At that size, they would really be too big to be called
weathervanes. As such, since they couldn't be made by the factory in Japan that was accustomed to
making such things, he had to start by searching for somewhere willing to manufacture them. As it
turned out, the skeletons and external skins were fabricated by an Italian factory that normally
makes ceilings, and the key rotating parts were contracted to another company that makes rides for
Euro Disney. Everything about this project was a first for Shingu, and he worried that it might not
go smoothly, but all the work was completed without any problems. When everything goes well,
that's because people work as a team, with everything directed towards the same objective. The
work was installed successfully, and the five sculptures each moved freely in the direction of the
wind, as if enjoying a dialogue with the clouds.

メリディアーナ・センター＋《雲との対話》　Meridiana Shopping Center and Offices + *Dialogue with Clouds*

Collaborations
06

レンゾ・ピアノ Renzo Piano

新宮 晋 Susumu Shingu

バンカ・ポポラーレ・ディ・ローディ ＋ 水の花
Banca Popolare di Lodi

Water Flower

中庭　Piazza

ロンバルディア州を代表する銀行、バンカ・ポポラーレ・ディ・ローディ本部のための建築物。元々この場所は鉄道駅に近い工業地帯で、ちょうどここにはチーズ製造工場と酪農場があった。こうした歴史的背景はサイロのような棟の形状に見られるように、建築設計の原動力となっている。軽量ガラスと細いスチール鋼によるキャノピー（天蓋型の庇）に覆われた大広場は建物の内側と外部を繋ぐ空間であり、銀行本部を訪れた人、ふらっと立ち寄った人、通り抜けする人など様々な町の人々が出会う場でもある。この大広場に新宮晋の彫刻がある。施設内にある800席を有する音楽ホールのロビーは大広場と連携しており、大広場は音楽ホールのロビーともなる。この地域の伝統的な建築材テラコッタを用いた開かれた建築空間は、町の一部として機能し溶け込んでいる。

This project was constructed as the headquarters of the Banca Popolare di Lodi, the leading bank of the Lombardy region. The area was originally an industrial zone near a railway station, with a cheese factory and dairy farm formerly situated at this particular site. The historical background of the area became the motive behind the design, as can be seen in the shape of the silo-like buildings. The large piazza covered by a canopy made of lightweight glass and thin steel ties is a space that connects the inside and outside of the building, and serves as a place where various people come together, including customers visiting the bank, people strolling through casually, and other passersby. A sculpture by Susumu Shingu is located in the large piazza. The lobby of the 800-seat auditorium located on site connects with the large piazza, which can also serve as part of the auditorium lobby. This open architectural space that incorporates terracotta, a traditional building material of the region, blends into, and functions as part of, the city.

PROJECT DATA	所在地	イタリア、ローディ	Location	Lodi, Italy
	デザイン・工期	1991-2001年	Design and Construction	1991-2001
	彫刻	1999年 制作	Sculpture	Produced in 1999

《水の花》(1999年)　*Water Flower*(1999)

ゼロからのスタート
Starting from zero

——— 新宮晋 Susumu Shingu

ミラノ近郊の街、ローディの街にある銀行の中庭に《水の花》は設置された。レンゾ・ピアノからの依頼内容は、「広大な中庭部分をガラスの庇で覆い、そこを銀行に用がなくても誰もが行き交うことができ、光と風が吹き抜ける心地いい空間にしたいので、その自然度をさらに高める水の作品を作って欲しい」ということだった。屋外空間に光と風を大胆に取り入れるピアノのコンセプトは、新宮にとっても大いに共感できるもので、アイデアはすぐに固まった。6対の半円形のカップが、次々と水を受けては流れ落ちていく設計で、設置後の中庭から聞こえる心地いい水の音は通り過ぎる人々の心を和ませ、この噴水だけを目当てに集まる人々があらわれるほど人気スポットになった。この《水の花》の彫刻で、関西国際空港プロジェクトで始まったピアノと新宮の公私にわたる付き合いは、およそ10年を迎えることになったが、二人のコラボレーションには馴れ合いやマンネリという言葉は無縁だ。プロジェクトごとにそれまでとは全然違う役割りをピアノは新宮に求める。新宮は、当然のことだが、いつものように全くのゼロからスタートする。それまでのやり方や経験に頼らない、新しい方法を考えて提案する。だから二人の共同作業には、いつも新鮮な緊張感がある。そうでなければ、何十年も続くわけがない。

Water Flower is installed in the inner piazza of a bank in the town of Lodi, a suburb of Milan. Renzo Piano wanted the piazza within the bank, a spacious plaza covered with a glass canopy accessible to everyone, even people who have no business with the bank, to be a light, airy, space that is a pleasant place to be, and asked Shingu to create a work involving water to make it feel even more natural. Piano's concept, with its bold incorporation of light and air in this outdoor space, struck a major chord with Shingu, and his idea quickly took shape. In his design, six semicircular cups are filled with water, one after the other, and then poured. Since its installation, the pleasant sound of this water coming from the inner piazza has soothed the hearts of passersby, and the location has become a popular spot, with people gathering just to see the fountain. This *Water Flower* sculpture was created after nearly a decade of public and private association between Piano and Shingu, which began with the Kansai International Airport project. But to describe their collaboration as having become cozy or stereotypical would be completely wrong. With each new project, Piano has asked Shingu to take on completely different roles. Naturally, Shingu starts afresh from zero each time, just as he always has. He thinks up and puts forward new ways of doing things, without relying on previous techniques or experiences. That is why joint projects between these two professionals always convey a vibrant tension. Were this not the case, they could not have continued for decades.

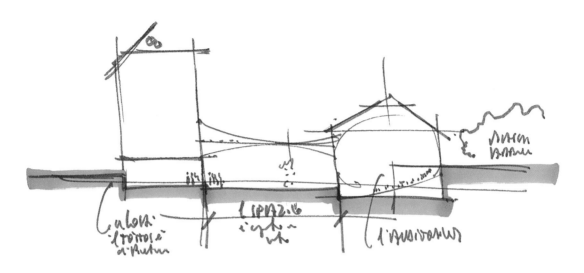

レンゾ・ピアノのスケッチ　Renzo Piano sketch

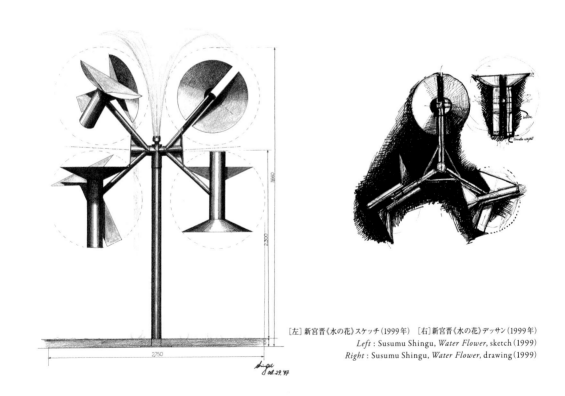

［左］新宮晋《水の花》スケッチ（1999年）　［右］新宮晋《水の花》デッサン（1999年）
Left : Susumu Shingu, *Water Flower*, sketch（1999）
Right : Susumu Shingu, *Water Flower*, drawing（1999）

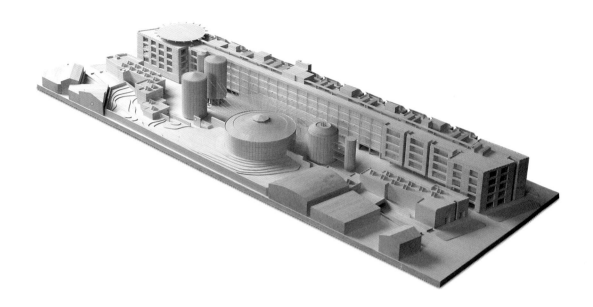

[左ページ 上]通りに面した外観
[左ページ 下]ガラスとスチール鋼によるキャノピー
[上]全体模型 1:200
[下]音楽ホール

Top of left page : Façade alongside the road
Bottom of left page : Canopy with lightweight glass and thin steel ties
Top : Overall model 1:200
Bottom : Auditorium

ガラスのキャノピーで覆われた中庭　Piazza cavered by the glass canopy

《水の花》（1999 年） *Water Flower*(1999)

レンゾ・ピアノ Renzo Piano

新宮 晋 Susumu Shingu

銀座メゾンエルメス ＋ 宇宙に捧ぐ
Ginza Maison Hermès

Hommage au Cosmos

銀座メゾンエルメス+《宇宙に捧ぐ》 ソニー通り側　Ginza Maison Hermès + *Hommage au Cosmos* from Sony Street

銀座にあるフランスのメゾン、エルメスの日本店舗兼オフィス、アトリエ、アート・ギャラリー。晴海通りに面して10m の幅しかなく、小径側に56mの奥行のある地上12階、地下3階建ての建物で、竣工当時は隣に同じく縦長の ソニービルがあった。56m幅のファサードの方に、最上部から新宮晋の彫刻が、ちょうど二つの棟が連なり 建物がセットバックした箇所に設置されている。建築を特徴づけるガラスのファサードには、エルメスのスカーフに ちなんでこの建物のために開発された45cm角の正方形のガラス製ブロックが1万3千個使われた。厳しい防火、 耐震規程に合わせて、各ガラスブロック間には4mmのあそびが設けられカーテンのように揺れを許容するよう 設計されている。半透明ガラスの覆いは、昼間は銀色に輝く。夜はランタンのように暖かい光でビル全体が覆われる。

The Japanese branch and offices for the French maison of Hermès in Ginza incorporates ateliers and an art gallery. Only 10m wide on its Harumi Avenue frontage, the building runs back 56m along a quiet side street (Sony Street), rising ten stories high above ground, with three levels below ground. At the time of its completion, a similarly long, narrow Sony building was located next door, across the side street. Sculpture work by Susumu Shingu hangs down from the top of the building, affixed to the very middle of the 56m façade, where it is set back from the street and the two halves of the building meet. The building's distinctive glass façade, inspired by the Hermès scarf, is made of 13,000 450mm-square glass blocks developed specially for this project. To meet stringent fire and earthquake regulations, the glass block façade is designed to sway like a curtain, with the flexible seals between the blocks allowing as much as 4mm of movement. By day, the translucent glass façade sparkles silver. By night, it covers the entire building in a warm light, resembling a lantern.

PROJECT DATA	所在地	日本、東京	Location	Tokyo, Japan
	デザイン・工期	1998-2006年	Design and Construction	1998-2006
	彫刻	2001年 制作	Sculpture	Produced in 2001

《宇宙に捧ぐ》(2001年)　*Hommage au Cosmos* (2001)

地上で最高のものを創る
Best in the world

——— ジャン゠ルイ・デュマ　Jean-Louis Dumas

90年代が終わる頃、ラグジュアリーメゾンのエルメスが東京・銀座にアート・ギャラリーやアトリエを含む日本の旗艦店を建てることになり、新宮晋はRPBWのパリオフィスに呼ばれた。打ち合わせには20人ほどが長いテーブルを囲んでいた。会議中、新宮の斜め向かいに座っていたエルメス社長（当時）のジャン゠ルイ・デュマは、こちらをちらちら見ながらずっと小さなノートにスケッチしていた。デュマは絵が上手かった。そして初対面の相手を描きながら、じっくり観察するのが好きだったようだ。地上で最高のものを創るというのはエルメスのモットーだったが、この哲学を確立したのはデュマだった。彼には商売人、実業家のイメージはほとんどなかった。まるで哲学者であり、アーティストだった。銀座のど真ん中に透き通ったようなガラスの軽い箱を置くようなイメージと、地上から宇宙に向かって光を発信する作品が生まれた。これは建築家のレンゾ・ピアノとクライアントのジャン゠ルイ・デュマ、それにアーティストの新宮晋ががっちり組んだコラボレーションの成果だ。その頃新宮が構想していた地球巡回プロジェクト「ウインドキャラバン」に共感したデュマは、各開催地にエルメスのスタッフを参加させ、資金的にも最後までこのプロジェクトを応援した。

Towards the end of the 1990s, when the luxury maison of Hermès decided to build a flagship store with an art gallery and ateliers in the Ginza district of Tokyo, Susumu Shingu was called to the Paris office of RPBW. The meeting involved around twenty people, gathered around a long table. The CEO of Hermès, Jean-Louis Dumas, was seated diagonally across the table from Shingu, and during the discussion he was constantly snatching glances at him and sketching in a small notebook. Dumas was an accomplished artist, and when meeting someone for the first time, liked to observe them closely and sketch them. Hermès's motto was to create the best on Earth, and it was Dumas who established this philosophy. There was almost nothing of the salesperson or businessman about him. He was altogether a philosopher and an artist.What emerged was the idea of placing a lightweight, transparent glass box in the very center of Ginza, and a work in which light is transmitted from Earth into space. This was the fruit of a robust collaboration formed between the architect Renzo Piano, the client Jean-Louis Dumas, and the artist Susumu Shingu. Dumas resonated with the global traveling exhibition *Wind Caravan* that Shingu was conceptualizing at that point, sent Hermès staff to take part at each site, and supported the project financially throughout.

レンゾ・ピアノと新宮晋　Renzo Piano and Susumu Shingu

［上］銀座メゾンエルメス+《宇宙に捧ぐ》 ソニー通り側の入口と地下鉄出口のある1階部分　［下左］晴海通りに面したショーウィンドウ　［下右］10階のテラス
Top : Ginza Maison Hermès + *Hommage au Cosmos*. Entrance on Sony Street, with integrated access to Metro.
Bottom left : Show window facing Harumi-dori　*Bottom right* : 10F terrace

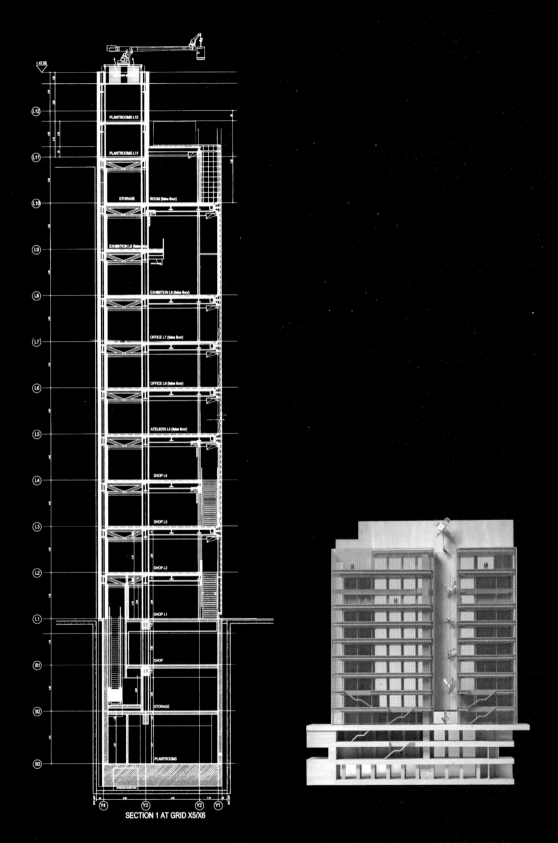

SECTION 1 AT GRID X5/X6

[左] 銀座メゾンエルメス　断面図　［右］銀座メゾンエルメス 全体模型（地層階含）1:100
Left : Ginza Maison Hermès cross section　*Right* : Ginza Maison Hermès overall model including floors below ground 1:100

竣工当時の晴海通りからの写真 右側はソニービル　Photo from Harumi-dori on completion. To the right is the Sony Building.

《宇宙に捧ぐ》(2001年)　*Hommage au Cosmos*(2001)

ソニービル解体後　北西側からの写真　Photo from north west side after Sony Building demolished

レンゾ・ピアノ Renzo Piano

新宮 晋 Susumu Shingu

イル・ソーレ24オーレ本社 ＋ 光の雲
"Il Sole 24 Ore" Headquarters   Cloud of Light

イル・ソーレ24オーレ本社 "Il Sole 24 Ore" Headquarters

RPBWはミラノの一地区に1960年代に建造されたビルを修復し、イタリアを代表する日刊経済新聞「イル・ソーレ24オーレ」の新本部へと改装する計画に携わった。モンテ・ローザ通り沿いのファサードを取り壊し、南側に開放部を新設、俯瞰するとU型のビルに変更したのである。中央の1万平米の広い中庭は、丘陵として構想された建築設計の中心となるスペースである。樫の木や灌木が植栽された緑が豊かに生い茂った丘の下には、450台もの車が収容可能な駐車場が作られた。また、中庭から13mの高さのアトリウムを通って大通りへと抜けることもできる。この吹き抜け空間に新宮晋の彫刻が天井から設置されている。新たなガラスのファサードには明るい緑色のブラインドが広範囲に設置された、緑溢れる雰囲気のビルである。

RPBW participated in this project to restore a building constructed in the 1960s in a district in Milan, and convert it into the new headquarters of the leading Italian financial daily newspaper *Il Sole 24 Ore*. By demolishing the facade facing Via Monte Rosa, a south-facing opening was created, creating a U-shape when viewed from above. A vast central garden covering 10,000sqm serves as a space forming the center of an architectural design conceived as a hill. A subterranean parking area capable of accommodating as many as 450 vehicles was built below the hill, which is lush with vegetation, planted with oak trees and shrubbery. The central garden offers access from the main road via a 13m-high atrium. A sculpture by Susumu Shingu hangs from the ceiling of this atrium space. The new glass façade was fitted with bright green blinds across a broad expanse, transforming the atmosphere of the building into one that is bright and full of green.

PROJECT DATA	所在地	イタリア、ミラノ	Location	Milan, Italy
	デザイン・工期	1998-2005年	Design and Construction	1998-2005
	彫刻	2004年 制作	Sculpture	Produced in 2004

《光の雲》（2004年）　*Cloud of Light*（2004）

作品を作るのではなく空間を創る
Create a space instead of making a work

——— 新宮晋 Susumu Shingu

広大な吹き抜け空間に設置され、あるかなきかのように24時間絶え間なく動く《光の雲》の軽やかな存在感は、吹き抜けを取り巻くオフィスで働く人々に潤いを与えているのではないだろうか。このスペースに《光の雲》があることで、建物と作品とが見事なハーモニーを創り出し、動きのある空間が生まれている。新宮のような彫刻作品を作るアーティストにとって、クライアントとの関係性は極めて重要だ。新宮は作品を依頼されたとき、いつもその場所、その空間に自分の作品が「あった方がいいのか」それとも「無くてもいいのか」を最初に考えるという。作品にストイックに向き合う姿勢は終始一貫している。クライアントとの関係とその重要性もまた、時間を経てからも変わらない。近年世界中に浸透している経済最優先の風潮の中で、作品を設置した時のクライアントが企業同士の合併や吸収でコロコロと変わり、その度に作品は当初のまま居続けられるのか分からない。この経済新聞社のビルでもいっとき風の流れが止められ、本来の作品の姿が失われた。それを見た新宮はビルのオーナーに掛け合い「24時間稼働のビルなのにどうして風だけが止まっているのか」と直談判をした。結果、しばらくして元の正常な動きを取り戻したという。いい場所、いいクライアント、そしていいタイミングが揃ってはじめて、人々を幸せにする最高の空間が生まれるのだ。

The unassuming presence of *Cloud of Light*, which is installed in an extensive atrium, and which moves continuously 24 hours a day in a visual game of "hide-and-seek," surely brings comfort to the people who work in the offices surrounding the atrium. Its presence in this space creates a perfect harmony between building and artwork, giving rise to a space full of movement.For an artist like Shingu who creates sculptural work the relationship with the client is of paramount importance. When a work is commissioned, Shingu first asks himself whether the space will be better for the presence of his artwork or whether it would do just as well without it. His attitude of stoicism when faced with his work is consistent from beginning to end. The importance of his relationship with the client also remains unchanged over time. With the modern world's pervasive tendency to prioritize economics above all else, corporate mergers and acquisitions mean that the client at the time a work is installed may end up changing later on, and the continued existence of the work itself may become uncertain. The flow of air in this financial newspaper's building was stopped temporarily, resulting in the essential nature of the artwork being lost. On seeing this, Shingu personally confronted the building's owners to ask why the air flow had been turned off in a building that operated twenty-four hours a day. As a result, it returned to its original normal movement a short while later. The creation of the ideal space for bringing people joy can only be achieved when the right site, the right client, and the right timing come together.

イル・ソーレ24オーレ本社+《光の雲》　"Il Sole 24 Ore" Headquarters + *Cloud of Light*

［上］丘陵状に隆起した中庭と駐車場入口
［右ページ 上］庇の部材（部分）
［右ページ 下］イル・ソーレ24オーレ本社　断面図

Top : Central garden hill with parking entrance
Top of right page : Canopy (detail)
Bottom of right page : "Il Sole 24 Ore" Headquarters cross section

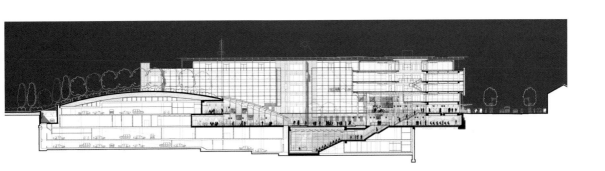

レンゾ・ピアノ Renzo Piano

新宮 晋 Susumu Shingu

スタヴロス・ニアルコス財団文化センター ＋ 宇宙、叙事詩、神話
Stavros Niarchos Foundation Cultural Center　Cosmos, Epic, Myth

運河側から見た人口丘と建物　Artificial hill and building viewed from the canal side

アテネから南に4kmの地点にあるカリテアに建設されたギリシャ国立図書館と国立オペラ劇場を有する巨大文化センターである。RPBWはこの地が古来から水と深い関係性があったことに着目し、海側に面して人口丘を作り、建物から海が眺められるようにした。人口丘は1：20の傾斜で、最も高い場所で地上から30mの高さがある。1万7千平米の広大な公園にはセンター入口へと続く遊歩道が作られている。建築を特徴付ける全面ソーラーパネルで覆われた100×100mの大きな庇状の屋根のすぐ下には図書館の読書室があり、360度ガラス壁面で覆われたこの部屋から、アテネと海の景観を眺めることができる。図書館と劇場はパブリックスペース「アゴラ」によって繋がれた。図書館と劇場、パブリックスペースにそれぞれ新宮晋の彫刻が合計3作品、天井から吊ってある。通常、オペラ劇場に設置されるシャンデリアに替えて、新宮の作品《宇宙》が優雅な動きを見せて観客の評判になっている。2016年10月グリーンビルディングのLEED最高賞であるプラチナ賞受賞。

This enormous cultural center comprising the National Library of Greece and the Greek National Opera House was constructed in Kallithea, 4km south of central Athens. Noting the area's strong relationship with the water since ancient times, RPBW created an artificial hill at the seaward end of the site, providing the site with spectacular views of the sea. The artificial hill rises at a 1:20 incline, reaching a height of 30m from ground level at its highest point. An esplanade was created in the expansive 170,000sqm park that leads to the entrance to the center. Directly below the distinctive canopy roof covered with a 100m × 100m array of photovoltaic cells lies an entirely glass-walled library reading room, providing a 360-degree view of Athens and the sea. The opera house and library are connected by a public space, known as the Agora. One sculpture each by Susumu Shingu is suspended from the ceiling in the opera house, library, and public space. Hanging from the ceiling of one of the halls in the opera house in place of the more typical chandelier, Shingu's *Cosmos* has become a sensation with visitors for its elegant movements. In October 2016, the complex obtained the LEED platinum certification, the Green Building Certification Institute's highest rating.

PROJECT DATA	所在地	ギリシャ、アテネ	Location	Athens, Greece
	デザイン・工期	2008-2016年	Design and Construction	2008-2016
	彫　刻	2016年 制作	Sculpture	Produced in 2016

《神話》(2016年)　*Myth*（2016）

時空を超えて

Beyond time and space

——— 新宮晋 Susumu Shingu

世界の海運王、スタヴロス・ニアルコスの名前が冠せられた壮大な文化複合施設は、2016年のオープン以来、ギリシャを代表する学術、アート、エンターテイメントの発信地になっている。アテネは新宮がローマに居た若い頃、訪ねたことのある思い出深い街だった。ヨーロッパ最古の文明が栄えた地のひとつで、西洋文明の源ともいえるギリシャには、新宮は多大な関心があったので、現地に入ってすぐにアクロポリスの丘にのぼりパルテノン神殿に向かった。先人たちが紡いできたギリシャの歴史に敬意を払いたかったからだ。この施設は、古代様式に従った現代版のアクロポリスで、文化・学術のための図書館と、芸能のための劇場とが一体となっている。それをつなぐのが広場（アゴラ）だ。この建築を特徴づける全面ソーラーパネルで覆われた100×100mの大きな庇状の屋根がどこからでも見えている。新宮がイメージしたのは、やって来る人たちの動線とその間の心理だった。日常生活から広場を横切って非日常な世界に入っていく心の変化を演出しようとした。古典の背表紙が圧倒的なボリュームで壁面を覆い尽くす国立図書館には《神話》、まるで大型シャンデリアのように新宮作品が吊るされたオペラハウス内には、ライブが始まるまでの時間をスペースアートの世界に誘う《宇宙》、そして、これから始まる舞台への高揚感を誘い、日常と非日常が切り替わるホワイエには《叙事詩》が設置された。

Since its opening in 2016, the magnificent Cultural Center named for the shipping magnate Stavros Niarchos has become one of Greece's most important centers for disseminating Greek learning, art, and entertainment. Shingu had visited Athens in his youth when he was living in Rome, and it was a city that held many memories for him. As the site where one of the oldest culture in Europe flourished, Greece can be described as the wellspring of Western culture; as such it held great interest for Shingu, and as soon as he arrived, he climbed the Acropolis and went straight to the Parthenon. He wanted to pay respect to the history of Greece that played out throughout the ages. This center is a contemporary version of the Acropolis following the ancient pattern, and combines a library for culture and learning and a theater for the arts in a single facility. These are connected by a plaza (*agora*). The huge, distinctive canopy-like roof covered with a 100m × 100m array of photovoltaic cells is visible throughout the complex.Shingu envisaged how visitors would flow through the site, and their frame of mind when doing so. He has tried to portray the change of feelings people experience as they cross the plaza, leaving behind the world of the ordinary and entering the world of the extraordinary.The National Library, the walls of which are almost entirely covered with the spines of an overwhelming number of classic books, contains Shingu's sculpture *Myth*. In the opera house, Shingu's work *Cosmos* hangs like a giant chandelier, inviting viewers into the world of space art during the time before the performance begins. And, *Epic* is installed in the foyer that forms the crossover between the mundane and the extraordinary, inducing a sense of elation at the performance that is about to start.

国立オペラ劇場ロビーの《叙事詩》　Susumu Shingu's *Epic* at lobby of the Greek National Opera auditorium

夕暮れ時　公園からの眺め　View from the park at dusk

国立オペラ劇場内部 俯瞰写真 2016年6月23日から26日のオープニングイベント時
Bird's eye view of the Greek National Opera auditorium during an opening event (June 23-26, 2016)

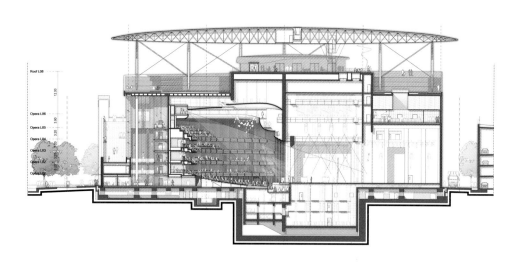

スタヴロス・ニアルコス財団文化センター 断面図
Stavros Niarchos Foundation Cultural Center cross section

国立オペラ劇場内部 《宇宙》
Cosmos in the Greek National Opera auditorium

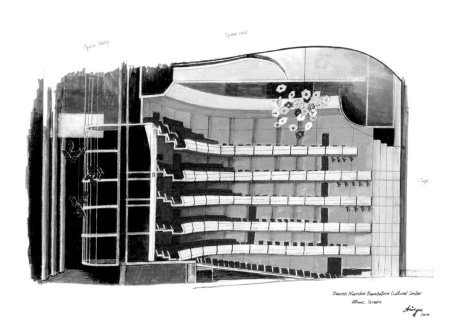

新宮晋《スタヴロス・ニアルコス財団文化センター》(2014年) 《宇宙》が天井から吊ってある
Susumu Shingu, *Stavros Niarchos Foundation Cultural Center. Cosmos* on the ceiling

ギリシャ国立図書館内部 《神話》 *Myth* in the National Library of Greece

レンゾ・ピアノ Renzo Piano

新宮 晋 Susumu Shingu

565ブルーム・ソーホー ＋ 虹色の葉
565 Broome SoHo　　　Rainbow Leaves

ファサード（部分）　Façade (detail)

565ブルーム・ソーホーはニューヨークのソーホー地区に建てられたRPBWによる高層マンションである。「565ブルーム」とは建物のある通りの名前。この地域は19世紀から20世紀にかけて建造された鋳鉄製のビル「カースト・アイアン」様式で特徴づけられる。ここに565ブルーム・ソーホーは21世紀建築の息吹を吹き込んだ。30階建ての建物からは、ハドソン川とニューヨークの景観が見渡せる。この建物の特徴は細いマリオンとファサードの曲線ガラスである。この二つの組み合わせがガラスのファサードを際立たせ、ビルの内と外の境界線を曖昧にして内部を光で満ち溢れさせる。このプロジェクトはRPBWとニューヨークのSLCE社（形態とファサードを担当）及びパリのデザイン会社RDAI社（インテリアデザインを担当）との協働による。

565 Broome SoHo is a high-rise condominium residence designed by RPBW located at 565 Broome Street in New York's Soho neighborhood. For SoHo, a district so closely identified with nineteenth and twentieth century cast-iron architecture, 565 Broome SoHo introduces an elegant twenty-first century inflection to the neighborhood. The 30-story structure provides sweeping views of the Hudson River and New York. Two notable aesthetic traits of this building are the mullions and the curved glass in the façade. The combination of the two makes the glass façade stand out, blurring the boundaries between inside and outside and filling the inside of the building with light.This project is a collaboration, on the one hand, between RPBW and the New York firm SLCE (in charge of both forms and façades), and on the other hand, the Paris design firm RDAI (in charge of the interior design).

PROJECT DATA	所在地	アメリカ、ニューヨーク	Location	New York, USA
	デザイン・工期	2014–2019年	Design and Construction	2014–2019
	彫刻	2021年 制作	Sculpture	Produced in 2021

《虹色の葉》（2021年）　*Rainbow Leaves*（2021）

クモは天才建築家
Spiders are genius architects

———— 新宮晋 Susumu Shingu

パンデミックが世界中を襲う前、まだ海外へも自由に往来ができた2019年夏に久々にニューヨークを訪れた新宮はRPBW・NYオフィスで相談を受けた。依頼内容は二つの建物をつないでひとつに見えるような作品を作って欲しいというものだった。今まで見ていた図面と現実のスペースとは全く違っていた。すでに出来上がっている建物に後から作品を考えるという、今までにないケースだった。しかし、あやとりや折り紙といった日本の伝統的な遊びを思い浮かべているうちに作品のコンセプトは固まった。フォルム、色の変化、そしてしなやかな動きを、この建物の住民だけでなく、街を行くニューヨーカーにも楽しんでもらおうと、作品名を《虹色の葉》(レインボー・リーブス)と名付け、プレゼンテーションを行った。新宮は「セントラルパークに舞う紅や黄色の落ち葉がクモの巣に引っかかっているイメージです」と説明し、それがクライアントやRPBWスタッフにも気に入られて、コロナ禍の中で制作作業は始まった。ほどなくイメージ通りに作品は仕上がったが問題は現地での据付けだった。通常なら現地に行き、指示を出しながら作業をするが、それが叶わない。現地の工事スタッフに理解されやすいよう設置方法を工夫し、何度も日本でテストを重ね運び出した。結果、知的な、まるでクモが巣を張るような作業だったが、リモートによる指示で見事に無事設置された。

In summer 2019, before the world was hit by the pandemic, when unrestricted international travel was still possible, Shingu revisited New York after an interval of some years, and called in at the RPBW New York office for a consultation. He had been asked to create a work that would connect two buildings so that they would appear to be a single structure. The plans he had previously seen were completely different from the actual space. Never before had he been faced with the task of coming up with an artwork for a building that had already been constructed. However, the concept took shape as he remembered the traditional Japanese pastimes of *ayatori* (a variety of cat's cradle) and *origami* paper folding. In his presentation, he named this work *Rainbow Leaves*, with the intention that not just the building's residents, but also New Yorkers heading into the city would be able to enjoy its changes in form and color, and its smooth movements. Shingu's explanation that it would evoke an image of the red and yellow fallen leaves of Central Park caught in a spider's web drew the approval of both the client and RPBW staff, and construction of the work began during the Covid-19 pandemic. Before too long, the work was ready as envisaged, but its installation on-site proved to be a problem. Normally, Shingu would go to the location and direct the work himself, but that was not possible this time. He had to devise an installation method that could be easily understood by the construction crew in New York, and sent the artwork off after numerous test runs in Japan. Consequently, the task was mentally challenging, like a spider weaving a web, but the work was installed successfully, thanks to his remote instructions.

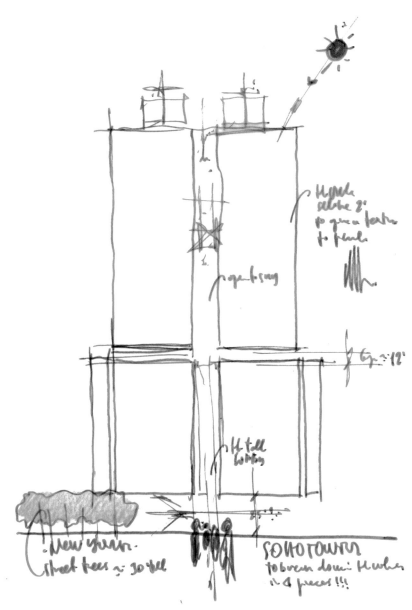

レンゾ・ピアノのスケッチ　Renzo Piano sketch

565ブルーム・ソーホー+《虹色の葉》　565 Broome SoHo + *Rainbow Leaves*

ハドソン川の眺め　View of the Hudson River

全体模型 1:100　Overall model 1:100

565ブルーム・ソーホー+《虹色の葉》
565 Broome SoHo + *Rainbow Leaves*

107

565 ブルーム・ソーホー +《虹色の葉》　565 Broome SoHo + *Rainbow Leaves*

屋内プール　Indoor pool

［左ページ］565ブルーム・ソーホー＋《虹色の葉》   *Left page* : 565 Broome SoHo + *Rainbow Leaves*
［上］《虹色の葉》（2021年）   *Top* : *Rainbow Leaves*（2021）

新宮晋と模型　新宮アトリエにて　Susumu Shingu With Models at Shingu Atelier

新宮 晋
ソロワーク

Susumu Shingu
Solo Work

大阪万博《フローティング・サウンド》
Expo '70 Osaka, *Floating Sound*

6年に及んだイタリア留学から帰国した翌年（1967年）、初めての野外彫刻展「風の造形」を東京・日比谷公園で開催した。日本美術界の仕組みも何も知らなかった新宮晋は、初めて自分の作品を発表する場所は東京のど真ん中、日比谷公園しかない！と考え、会場を確保するための煩雑な許認可申請など全てのお膳立てを自ら整えた。この頃から「風のアーティスト」新宮晋の物語が幕を開けるのだが、この日比谷の展覧会は評判を呼び、大阪万博を彩る彫刻作品を作る7人の野外彫刻作家の一人に選ばれた。会場中心の「進歩の湖」の湖上に浮かび、音と波が現代音楽のように自在にシンクロする発表作は、他の作家たちとは全く異質だった。自身も述懐するように、この大阪万博がなかったら新宮の後の活躍はなかっただろう。

In 1967, the year after his return to Japan after six years of study in Italy, Shingu organized his first solo outdoor sculpture exhibition, *Wind Structures*, at Hibiya Park in Tokyo. Completely unaware of how the art world generally worked in Japan, Shingu decided that this high-profile spot in the center of Tokyo would be the perfect place for his first exhibition, and made all the arrangements himself, including the complex procedures involved in getting permission to exhibit in a public park. Ever since, he has been known as a sculptor of the wind. This amazing debut in Hibiya was a hit, and before long, he was one of seven sculptors selected to create open-air sculptures for Expo '70 in Osaka. *Floating Sound* was placed on the Lake of Dreams, where the ripples and sounds produced by his sculptures played in concert, synchronized like contemporary music. The result was completely unlike that of any of the other sculptors' works. Looking back, Shingu is convinced that his career would not have taken off without the Expo project.

「せんい館」の隣にあったスイス館の傍の湖に、白と黄各3体を交互に輪状につなげ浮かべた作品。一体に一本ずつ渡されたバーの端には片方にスプーン状の柄杓、反対側に三角錐の形をした重りが付けられている。ポンプで湖から吸い上げて送られた水で柄杓がいっぱいになるとバーが傾き柄杓の中の水が湖に戻る。すると、今度はバーの重り側が下がって、三角錐の底辺が水面を叩いて波紋が拡がって音を響かせる仕組み。

On the lake alongside the Swiss Pavilion, which was next to the Textiles Pavilion, Shingu linked three white and three yellow floating structures in a circle, with the colors alternating. Each had a bar mounted on top, with a spoon-shaped receptacle at one end and a triangular pyramid weight suspended from the other end. A pump drew up water from the lake and sent it along the bar to the spoon. When the spoon filled up, the bar tilted and released the water back into the lake. The weight at the other end then descended, tilting the bar the other way so that the base of the triangular pyramid slapped the surface of the lake, making a sound and sending out waves.

《フローティング・サウンド》（1970年）
Floating Sound（1970）

PROJECT DATA

所在地	日本、大阪
制作年	1970年

Location	Osaka, Japan
Production	1970

スイス館「光の木」と《フローティング・サウンド》　*The Tree of light* (Swiss Pavillion) and *Floating Sound*

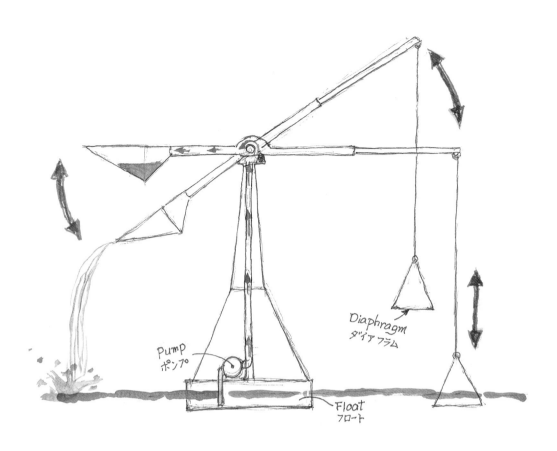

Pump
ポンプ

Diaphragm
ダイア フラム

Float
フロート

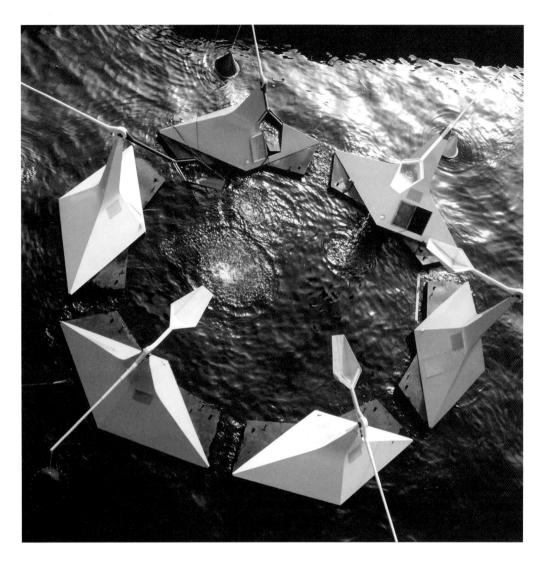

[左ページ 上]《フローティング・サウンド》スケッチ（1970年）　　　　Top of left page : Floating Sound, sketch (1970)
[左ページ 下]《フローティング・サウンド》（1970年）　　　　　　　　Bottom of left page : Floating Sound (1970)
[上]《フローティング・サウンド》（1970年）　　　　　　　　　　　　Top : Floating Sound (1970)
[下]《フローティング・サウンド》スケッチ（1970年）　　　　　　　　Bottom : Floating Sound, sketch (1970)

雑創の森　風車・風見
Zasso Forest School, Windmill and Wheathervane

ある日、大阪・能勢の山奥にあった新宮のアトリエに突然長身の青年が訪ねてきた。「今ぼくは理想の幼稚園を計画しています。そこにはどうしても新宮さんの彫刻が欲しいんです」。そして彼は、自然の中で子どもたちを遊ばせながらのびのび育てるという、彼の理想の教育論を一気に話し始めた。奈良と京都の県境にある山中に建設予定の大プロジェクトで、とてもこの青年一人で実現出来る話とは思えなかった。それで「建築家は誰?」と尋ねると六角鬼丈だと言う。新宮は、六角氏とは以前に仕事をしたこともあり、気心の知れた仲だった。クライアントの小笠原浩方が一番若く、建築家の六角も新宮も皆30代。最初のイメージ作りから率直な意見が交わされた。アートと建築を一体化した7つの塔の上に1体ずつ大きな風見が乗るデザインが決まった。この建物は、国内外でも高く評価され、1979年吉田五十八賞の「建築に貢献したアートの部」と「建築の部」の両賞を独占した。

On day, a tall young man turned up at Shingu's studio deep in the hills to the north of Osaka. "I'm designing the ideal kindergarten, and your sculptures need to be part of it," he announced, then launched into an explanation of his thoughts on education, which involved children growing at their own pace through play, surrounded by nature. The kindergarten was a large project for a site in the range of hills separating Nara and Kyoto. Shingu doubted that the young man could pull it off by himself, and asked "Who is the architect?" "Kijo Rokkaku," was the answer. Shingu had worked with Rokkaku before, and knew him well. The client, Hirokata Ogasawara, was the youngest in a team of thirty-somethings, including Rokkaku and Shingu. Fervent discussion of ideas began with the first attempts to create an image of what was needed. Eventually, they settled on a design that integrated art and architecture, topping each of seven towers with a large weathervane. The building attracted substantial acclaim from around the world, and locked out the *Yoshida Isoya Prize* awards in 1979, winning both the Art in Architecture section and the Architecture section.

「雑創の森」(現・そよかぜ幼稚園)は1977年京都府京田辺市に設立された幼稚園舎。20世紀初頭に活躍したドイツの哲学者ルドルフ・シュタイナーの思想をベースに理想の幼稚園を目指して設立された。うっそうと生い茂る木々に囲まれた森の中の敷地に建てられた白い現代建築の高低差のある棟の上に設置された7体の風見と三角屋根の天辺に据えられた1体の赤い風車が新宮晋の彫刻である。

The Zasso Forest School project involved the building for a kindergarten established in Kyotanabe in Kyoto Prefecture in 1977 (now renamed the Soyokaze Kindergarten). The aim was to create a kindergarten on principles derived from the ideas of Rudolf Steiner, a German philosopher of the early twentieth century. The site was within a forest, surrounded by dense growth of trees. The buildings were modern designs in white, with a variety of heights. The seven weathervanes on the tops of the towers, plus one red windmill, are all Shingu sculptures.

雑創の森　スケッチ (1977年)
Zasso Forest School, sketch (1977)

PROJECT DATA

所在地	日本、京都
制作年	1977年

Location	Kyoto, Japan
Production	1977

雑創の森（1977年）　Zasso Forest School（1977）

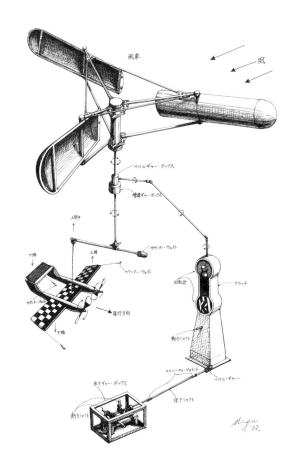

［左ページ 上］雑創の森　デッサン（1977年）
［左ページ 下］雑創の森　風車
［上］風車小屋の内部

Top of left page : Zasso Forest School, drawing (1977)
Bottom of left page : Zasso Forest School, Windmill
Top : Zasso Forest School, Interior of Windmill

世界巡回野外彫刻展「ウインドサーカス」
World Traveling Exhibition of Outdoor Sculptures, *Windcircus*

「ウインドサーカス」は、風で動く彫刻作品10点と共にヨーロッパ4都市とアメリカ5都市を2年かけて巡回した。新宮は50歳を迎え、改めて「アートとは何か？ 僕のやっていることが本当にアートなのか？」という根本命題が頭に浮かんだ。「美術館にもめったに来ないような普通の人たちが、日常生活の中で突然アートに出会ったら、どんな反応をするのだろう？」という問いの答えを求めて、海外に飛び出した。巡回展のつもりが、最初に決まっていたのはドイツのブレーメンだけだった。ブレーメンの会期中にスペインのバルセロナから声が掛かり、続けてイタリアのフィレンツェ、フィンランドのラハティと、ヨーロッパの4都市を巡り、翌年にはニューヨークを皮切りにロサンゼルスまで、アメリカの5都市を巡回した。勝手の分からない外国の街で、どこに作品を設置できるのか不安もあったが、後は持ち前のポジティブ・シンキングが全てを解決へ導いてくれる。新宮は言った「やって良かったぁ」。

For Windcircus, Shingu traveled with ten wind-activated sculptures, presenting his exhibition in four European cities and five cities in America within a two-year period. Having reached his fifties, Shingu found himself thinking about the fundamental issue of whether what he was doing was really art. Pondering the question of "If ordinary people who rarely go to art museums suddenly encountered art in their everyday lives, how would they react?" he set off into the world to find an answer. Shingu planned a traveling exhibition, but when he started, only one venue had been fixed, the German city of Bremen. Nevertheless, during the exhibition at Bremen he was invited to Barcelona. Later, he added Firenze in Italy, and Lahti in Finland, resulting in a four-city tour of Europe. The following year he traveled around America, where he exhibited in five cities, beginning in New York and ending in Los Angeles. In countries where he was unaccustomed to how things are done, he was not sure where he would be able to set up his exhibition, but his characteristic positive thinking eventually found solutions to all the issues that cropped up. He emerged from the project saying, "I'm glad I did it!"

1987年5月10日から1989年1月21日まで欧米で行われた彫刻作品の野外展示ツアー。1987年はヨーロッパ4都市を、1988年6月1日からアメリカ5都市を回った。ブレーメンではマルクト広場に世界遺産に登録された市庁舎を前に、バルセロナではインドゥストリアル公園の湖の中に、ニューヨークでは世界貿易センター広場に展示されるなど、その町に応じた多様な展示がなされた。

This was an outdoor sculpture exhibition that toured Europe and America from May 10, 1987 to January 21, 1989. After presenting the exhibition at four cities in Europe in 1987, it went on to visit five cities in the US, beginning on June 1, 1988. The exhibition venues varied greatly from city to city, enabling him to adapt the exhibition to local circumstances. At Bremen, he set up his sculptures in the Marktplatz in front of the Town Hall, which has been recognized as a World Heritage site. In Barcelona, he installed them in the lake in the Parc de l'Espanya Industrial, and in New York, he presented them in the Plaza at the World Trade Center.

「ウインドサーカス」スペイン、バルセロナ（1987年）
Windcircus, Barcelona, Spain (1987)

PROJECT DATA

所在地	世界9都市
活動年	1987-1989年

Location	9 cities around the world
Project	1987-1989

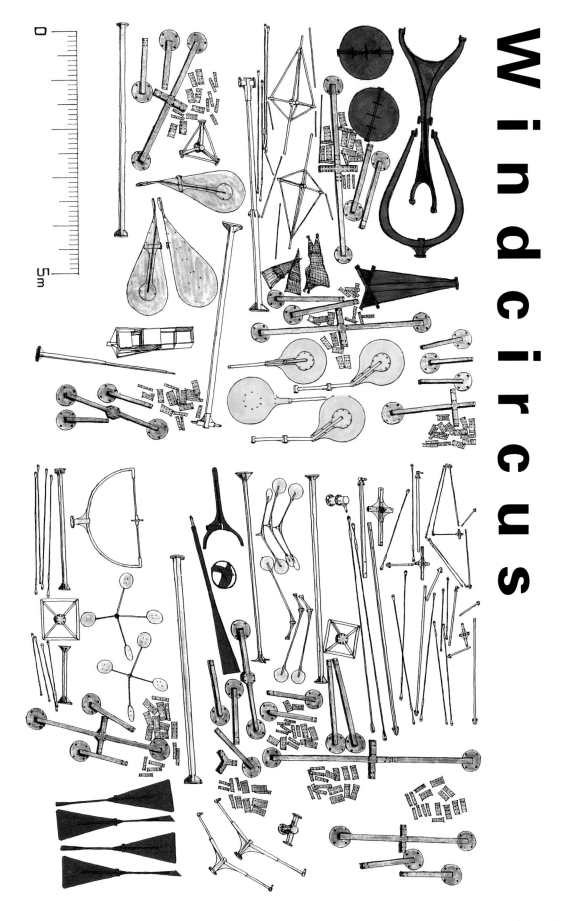

W i n d c i r c u s

「ウインドサーカス」スケッチ（1987-1989年）　　*Windcircus*, sketch (1987-1989)

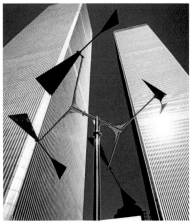

「ウインドサーカス」　［左］フィンランド、ラハティ　［右上］アメリカ、ロサンゼルス　［右下］アメリカ、ニューヨーク
Windcircus　*Left* : Lahti, Finland　*Top right* : Los Angeles, USA　*Top right bottom* : New York, USA

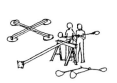

「ウィンドサーカス」デッサン　*Windcircus*, drawing

作品は分解された状態で運ばれ、現地で組み立てられた
The work was transported disassembled and assembled on site.

世界巡回プロジェクト「ウインドキャラバン」
World Traveling Project, *Wind Caravan*

50代で「ウインドサーカス」を実行し、確かな方向性を感じとった新宮は、60代に入りもっと地球のことを知りたいという思いが募り「ウインドキャラバン」プロジェクトを敢行した。目的地を定めるため、時には慣れない四駆で現地を走り回ったりして都合2年をかけて世界各地をロケハンした。その結果、厳しい自然環境が避けられない僻地6カ所を選び、21点の彫刻と風車小屋を詰めた6mのコンテナと共に訪ねて各地で交流を図った。地元、三田の田んぼからスタートし、ニュージーランドの無人島、フィンランドの凍結湖、モロッコの岩山、モンゴルの大草原、ブラジルの砂丘と2年をかけて巡回した。それぞれの土地に暮らす先住民とは言葉も肌の色も全く違うのに、心と心が通じて冗談を言い合い、お互い涙が出るほど笑えたのは、私たちの先祖が5万年ほど前南アフリカに生まれ、様々な事情で世界中に広がっていった、元は一家族だという証拠だと思った。※

Organizing and producing *Windcircus* in his fifties gave Shingu a sense of direction, and as he entered his sixties he realized that he wanted to know more about the world. This led to his ambitious *Wind Caravan* project. To decide on the destinations for the tour, he spent two years checking out potential locations around the world, sometimes having to resort to four-wheel drive to get to where he needed to go. Eventually, he selected six isolated locations where the effects of a tough natural environment were unavoidable. Packing twenty-one sculptures and the windmill house into a 6m shipping container, he traveled with the container and planned to get to know local people at each venue. The first venue was a stepped rice field in Sanda, Japan. This was followed by an uninhabited island in New Zealand, a frozen lake in Finland, rocky hills in Morocco, the steppes in Mongolia, and sand dunes in Brazil, taking two years overall. The indigenous people he met in the communities he visited each had different appearances and spoke different languages, but wherever he went, he discovered kindred hearts and minds with whom he could share jokes and laugh so much that both parties cried. He saw it as proof that we are all part of the same family, with our ancestors originating in southern Africa some 50,000 years ago before spreading throughout the world under a variety of circumstances.※

2000年6月12日日本・三田から始まり2001年12月2日ブラジル・クンブーコまで実施された21点の野外彫刻と風車小屋を展示して回ったツアー。三田では田んぼのあぜ道に、フィンランドの町イナリでは雪や凍った湖に、モロッコのタムダハトでは乾いた土の高原などを会場に、折り畳み式の旗状の彫刻がその土地、その土地に応じて多彩に展開され、人々とのかけがえのない交流が生まれた。

This was a tour of an exhibition comprising twenty-one outdoor sculptures and a windmill house, which traveled the world beginning at Sanda, Japan on June 12, 2000, and finishing at Cumbuco in Brazil on December 2, 2001. The venues ranged from the paths between rice paddies at Sanda, to snow and a frozen lake at Inari in Finland, and the dry soil of the hilltops at Tamdagh in Morocco. Adapting the flag-like sculptures with their folding sails to fit the land in each locality was a precious opportunity for people of very different backgrounds to get to know each other.

「ウインドキャラバン」ニュージーランド、モトコレア（2000年）
Wind Caravan, Motukorea, New Zealand (2000)

PROJECT DATA

所在地	地球上の特異な自然空間6カ所
活動年	2000-2001年

Location	6 unique natural spaces on earth
Project	2000-2001

※ 諸説あります。Various theories exist.

「ウインドキャラバン」モンゴル、ウンドルドブ（2001年）　*Wind Caravan*, Undur Dov, Mongolia（2001）

「ウインドキャラバン」ブラジル、クンブーコ（2001年）　*Wind Caravan*, Cumbuco, Brasil（2001）

日本、三田　Sanda, Japan

モロッコ、タムダハト　Tamedakhte, Morocco

ニュージーランド、モトコレア　Motukorea, New Zealand

フィンランド、イナリ
Inari, Finland

モンゴル、ウンドルドブ
Undur Dov, Mongolia

モロッコ、タムダハト
Tamedakhte, Morocco

日本、三田　Sanda, Japan

ブラジル、クンブーコ
Cumbuco, Brasil

ニュージーランド、モトコレア
Motukorea, New Zealand

モンゴル、ウンドルドブ　Undur Dov, Mongolia

フィンランド、イナリ　Inari, Finland

ブラジル、クンブーコ　Cumbuco, Brasil

［上］「ウインドキャラバン」フィンランド、イナリ（2001年）
［左下］「ウインドキャラバン」モンゴル、ウンドルドブ（2001年）
［右下］「ウインドキャラバン」ニュージーランド、モトコレア（2000年）

Top : Wind Caravan, Inari, Finland (2001)
Bottom left : Wind Caravan, Undur Dov, Mongolia (2001)
Bottom right : Wind Caravan, Motukorea, New Zealand (2000)

「呼吸する大地（ブリージング・アース）」プロジェクト
The project, *Breathing Earth*

「ウインドサーカス」から「ウインドキャラバン」へと数年を費やした二つのプロジェクトを経て、70歳台に入った新宮は「人間は地球に優しく生きていかなければいけない」とますます強く思うようになった。「地球をこれ以上傷めずに生きて行く方法を考えなくてはならない。そこにはきっとアートの力が必要だ」。行き着いた答えのひとつが風力や太陽光といった自然エネルギーで自活する村「呼吸する大地（ブリージング・アース）」プロジェクトだ。新宮晋の壮大な夢でもある。ドイツ人映画作家トーマス・リーデルスハイマーは、この夢の実現に世界中を駆け巡る新宮を6年間に渡って密着取材し、ドキュメンタリー映画『ブリージング・アース―新宮 晋の夢』を作り世界各国で数々の映画賞を受賞した。

Some time after spending several years on the *Windcircus* and *Wind Caravan* projects, Shingu entered his seventies, becoming increasingly convinced that humanity must live in a way that is kind to the earth. "We have to find ways to live that don't damage our world further. The power of art surely has an essential role." One solution that he found was the *Breathing Earth* project for a self-sufficient village using natural energy sources like wind and solar. German video artist Thomas Riedelsheimer spent several years with Shingu as he traveled the world in order to make this dream a reality. This resulted in Riedelsheimer's documentary *Breathing Earth – Susumu Shingu's Dream*, which received film awards in many countries.

2009年から10年にかけて、足利工業大学の風力発電実験として兵庫県芦屋市潮芦屋ビーチに高さ8m・回転直径7mもの巨大な風車の実寸プロトタイプを組立て設置したのを皮切りに、2011年には田植えから刈り取りまでの4カ月間の期間、田んぼに野外彫刻を設置し子どもたちを招いて大地の鼓動を感じるプロジェクト「田んぼのアトリエ」を実施。ブリージング・アースの発電風車《里山風車》は、2013年から「新宮晋 風のミュージアム」に常設されている。

Shingu's experiments for *Breathing Earth* began by assembling and installing a full-size windmill prototype with a height of 8m and a diameter of 7m in Hyogo Prefecture at the southern tip of Shioashiya Beach in the Minamiashiya Hama district. This was an Ashikaga University wind power experiment that ran for ten years beginning in 2009. Then, in 2011, his *Atelier in the Rice Paddies* project ran for four months from planting time to harvesting, as a place where children could sense the land changing over the seasons, with outdoor sculptures installed in the paddies. A *Breathing Earth* wind generator (*Satoyama Windmill*) has been installe

「呼吸する大地」スケッチ（2010年）
Breathing Earth, sketch (2010)

PROJECT DATA

所在地	日本、兵庫
活動年	2009年 -

Location	Hyogo, Japan
Project	2009 -

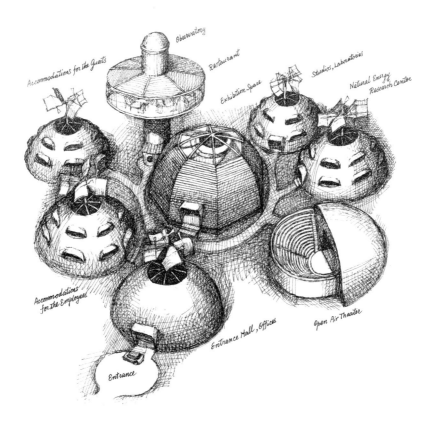

「呼吸する大地」デッサン（2010年）　*Breathing Earth*, drawing（2010）

「呼吸する大地」デッサン（2010年）　*Breathing Earth*, drawing（2010）

「呼吸する大地」スケッチ（2014年）　*Breathing Earth*, sketch（2014）

「呼吸する大地」ジオラマ（2009年）　*Breathing Earth*, Diorama (2009)

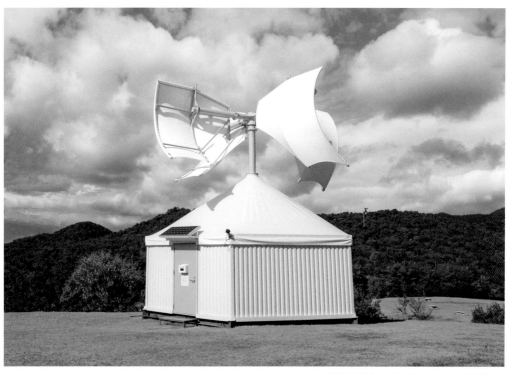

《里山風車》（2013年）　*Satoyama Windmill* (2013)

兵庫県立有馬富士公園「新宮晋 風のミュージアム」

Arimafuji Park, "Susumu Shingu Wind Museum"

森と湖に囲まれ、恵まれた自然環境の中にこの「新宮晋 風のミュージアム」は存在する。風や水といった自然エネルギーで動く作品を作り続けて来た新宮が、代表作12点を兵庫県に寄贈して2014年にオープンした。誕生のきっかけは2009年の大晦日。その日は雪が降っていた。たまたま三田の新宮のところで大晦日を一緒に過ごそうと訪ねていたフランスのインテリア・デザイナー、ペルネット・ペリアンに日本の雪景色を見せたいと思い、近くの県立有馬富士公園へ案内した。その時、動物の足跡ひとつない、すっぽり雪におおわれた一角を見つけた。周囲を森に囲まれたその場所は、「自分の彫刻たちにぴったりだ」と新宮は思った。それから暫くして当時の県知事に会う機会があり、作品が配置された完成イメージ図を見せた。それから話はトントン拍子で進み、夢のようなミュージアムが誕生した。

The Susumu Shingu Wind Museum is a museum devoted to outdoor sculpture. Including an individual artist's name in the name of the facility is very unusual for public parks in Japan. Susumu Shingu has long been creating works that use the natural energy of wind or water to move, and the museum opened in 2014 with Shingu's donation to Hyogo Prefecture of twelve of his best-known wind sculptures. The idea came to him on New Year's Eve in 2009, when the French interior designer Pernette Perriand visited him in Sanda. Shingu decided to show him a Japanese snowscape, and took him to the nearby Arimafuji Park. They found an area of the park that was blanketed cleanly with snow, without even any animal tracks. It was surrounded by trees, and Shingu had the revelation that it would be an ideal place for his sculptures. Some time later, Shingu had the opportunity to meet the governor of Hyogo Prefecture, and showed him a rendering of what the park could look like with the sculptures. After that, the idea progressed smoothly, and before long, the sort of museum that you usually only dream about was born.

兵庫県三田市にある兵庫県立都市公園、有馬富士公園内「休養ゾーン」に「新宮晋 風のミュージアム」はある。有馬富士公園の面積は178.2ヘクタールの広域に及ぶ森林と緑地、池を含む一帯。2001年北側の「出合いのゾーン」開園に始まり、2007年「休養ゾーン」へと範囲を拡大し、2009年第1区域全体が開園した。この後、2014年に「休養ゾーン」内に開園したのが「新宮晋 風のミュージアム」である。緑の広場とビオトープ池に新宮晋の12点の野外彫刻が設置されている。

The Susumu Shingu Wind Museum is situated in the Recreation Zone within Hyogo Arimafuji Park, a city park operated by Hyogo Prefecture in Sanda City. The Arimafuji Park is a sizable 178.2 hectares, and within this broad expanse of land are forested areas, green areas, and a lake. An Encounter Zone opened in 2001 on the north side of the park, and in 2007 it expanded to become a Recreation Zone. In 2009, the entire Phase 1 area opened. The Susumu Shingu Wind Museum was established in 2014 within the Recreation Zone. There are now 12 outdoor sculptures by Shingu installed on the lawn and in the biotope pond.

WIND MUSEUM
Susumu Shingu

PROJECT DATA

所在地	日本、兵庫
制作年	2014年

Location	Hyogo, Japan
Production	2014

「新宮晋 風のミュージアム」俯瞰写真 (2014年)　Susumu Shingu Wind Museum, bird's eye view (2014)

〈双子星〉 *Astral Twins* (1986)

《風のロンド》 *Rond of the Wind* (2014)

《すい星》 *Comet* (1987)

《宇宙の翼》 *Cosmic Wings* (1999)

《風の結晶》 *Wind Crystal* (1986)

《白い肖像II》 *White Portrait II* (1988)

《ソアリング》 *Soaring* (2008)

《星座》 *Constellation* (1986)

《シグナル》 *Signal* (2008)

《スペースグラフィティ》 *Space Graffiti* (1986)

《時の木》 *Time Tree* (1988)

《気まぐれな時計》 *Capricious Clock* (1987)

《里山風車》 *Satoyama Windmill* (2013)

新宮晋　模型
Susumu Shingu's models

これらは、精巧に作られた小型彫刻作品であり、野外彫刻制作の前に試作されるものでもある。1980年代から今日まで制作されたこれらの模型は他ならぬ新宮アトリエにある。様々な場所へ旅立って風や光を感じさせる彫刻の原型である色とりどりの模型が来訪者を迎え、回りながら夢の世界の入口へと誘ってくれる。

Models are carefully fabricated small sculptures, functioning as prototypes prepared in advance of the creation of outdoor sculptures. These models, made from the 1980s onwards, could only be seen at the studio of Susumu Shingu.Colorful models that are the original forms of sculptures sent out to make viewers aware of the wind and light in their various destinations provide a welcome, clattering around and drawing visitors into the entrance of a dream world.

《光の鼓動》
Light-Beat
(1995)

《詩の翼》
Wing of Poetry
(2018)

《海のシンフォニー》
Symphony of the sea
(2005)

《プロポーザル》
Proposal
(1996)

《海の響き》
Resonance of the sea
(1995)

《プロポーザル》
Proposal
(1990)

《生命の惑星》
Planet of Life
(1997)

《波の記憶》
Memory of the Waves
(1994)

《大地の翼》
Wings of the Earth
(2005)

《太陽のあいさつ》
Greetings of the Sun
(2005)

《プロポーザル》
Proposal
(2013)

《星のシグナル》
Astral Signal
(1996)

《プロポーザル》
Proposal
(1996)

《風の記憶》
Memory of Wind
(2002)

《プロポーザル》
Proposal
(2005)

《雪の翼》
Snow Wings
(2018)

《プロポーザル》
Proposal
(2006)

《帆走する雲》
Sailing Clouds
(1996)

《太陽の神話》
Myth of the Sun
(1994)

《森の伝説》
Legend of the Forest
(1998)

《プロポーザル》
Proposal
(2013)

《太陽の肖像》
Portrait of the Sun
(1997)

《色彩の響き》
Resonance of Colors
(1981)

《プロポーザル》
Proposal
(2022)

《プロポーザル》
Proposal
(2002)

《星のこだま》
Echo of Stars
(1995)

《星の対話》
Astral Dialogue
(2017)

《光る風》
Luminous Wind
(1999)

《風景の記憶》
Memory of Landscape
(2000)

《波の翼》
Wing of the Waves
(1991)

新宮 晋 室内作品 Susumu Shingu's Indoor Works

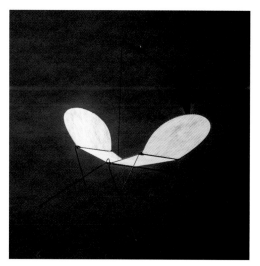

《自由の翼》 *Wings of Freedom* (2014)

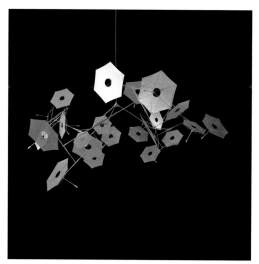

《小さな宇宙》 *Little Cosmos* (2014)

《空のこだま》 *Echo of Sky* (2016)

《おいかけっこ》 *Catch and Run* (2022)

かすかな微風にも動く「グラム彫刻」と新宮晋が名付けた彫刻作品の数々は、グラム単位で精密に設計された彫刻作品である。ゆったりとした動きで光を反射し、室内に思いもかけぬ影を落とす。空間そのものの質を高め、濃密にし、作品が置かれた場所には静謐な時が流れる。わずかに動くだけで、静寂の中に弦楽器の弦やピアノの鍵盤がはじかれて美しい音色を鳴り響かせるかのように、作品の置かれた空間全体と時間を、永遠に続く普遍的な何ものかに変えてしまう魔法を秘めた彫刻である。

The many sculptural works named "gram sculptures" by Susumu Shingu that move even in the slightest breeze have been designed with precision to the nearest gram. Installed indoors, their leisurely movements reflect the light and cast unexpected shadows. They heighten the quality of the space itself and condense it, and time flows peacefully wherever they are placed. These sculptures hold an inherent magic, as their slightest movements transform the entire space and time in which they are situated into something eternal and universal, as if the strings of a violin or the keys of a piano were to burst into lovely music out of a hushed silence.

《月の舟 NY》 *Moon Boat NY* (2022)

《雲の日記》 *Diary of Clouds* (2016)

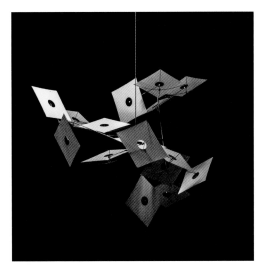

《星空》 *Starry Night* (2013)

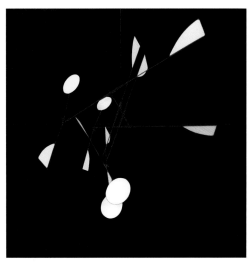

《La Pace》 *La Pace* (2017)

レンゾ・ピアノ　RPBWの工房にて　2016年　Renzo Piano in the studio at RPBW in 2016

レンゾ・ピアノ
ソロワーク

Renzo Piano
Solo Work

ポンピドー・センター

Centre Georges Pompidou

1969年仏大統領ジョルジュ・ポンピドーが文化センター設立を発案し、1971年フランス文化省による設計競技が行われた。レンゾ・ピアノはリチャード・ロジャースと組んで参加、見事勝者となった。パリ中心部の歴史的建造物が立ち並ぶマレ地区に位置するなだらかな台地の地名から「ボーブール」とも呼ばれる。上7層、地下3層建ての建物の構造体はスチールで、なかでも横48mのワーレントラスとダイキャストスチール「ガーベレット」によって内部の広く柔軟性に富む空間が確保されている。外観の色とりどりのチューブは剥き出しのダクトであり、青が空気、緑が水、黄色が電気、赤がエレベーター、エスカレーターの移動系統。エスカレーターもファサードに面した構造体の一部となっており、その前衛性は世界を震撼させた。2000年リニューアルオープン時の改装もRPBWによる。

This project was conceived in 1969 by French President Georges Pompidou, and in 1971, the French Ministry of Culture launched an international design competition. Renzo Piano, entering the competition with Richard Rogers, surprised many by winning. The site is the Plateau Beaubourg, a gently-sloping rise in the Marais, a district of central Paris packed with historical buildings. Constructed with seven stories above ground and three underground, it is a steel frame structure incorporating 48m warren trusses mounted on die-cast steel "gerberette" to provide expansive internal spaces that ensure flexibility. Outside, its ducts are exposed color-coded tubes. Blue tubes carry air, green tubes carry water, yellow tubes are for electricity cables. and red tubes are for vertical circulation, containing escalators and elevators. The elevators face the façade and are part of the structure. This radical design was a shock that shook the world. When renovation works were required, they were also handled by RPBW, enabling the Centre to reopen in 2000.

当時レンゾ・ピアノはこの建物の建築家だと言った途端、パリの老婦人から傘で殴られそうになったという。それほど前衛的だった。古くからのパリの濃密な街並みを破壊したと批判されたという。このプロジェクトで、レンゾ・ピアノはこの先彼が亡くなる1992年までパートナーシップを築く優秀な構造家ピーター・ライス（オーヴ・アラップ社）と知り合った。

The extremely avantgarde nature of the building provoked strong emotions. When Renzo Piano told a woman he was talking to that he was its designer, she apparently hit him with her umbrella. The building was criticized for destroying part of the dense urban fabric of old Paris, but it also attracted enormous acclaim. It was through this project that Renzo Piano came to know the talented structural engineer Peter Rice of Ove Arup & Partners, and they continued to work in partnership until Rice's death in 1992.

ノートルダム大聖堂から見た改装時の写真
Under renovation, seen from Notre-Dame de Paris

PROJECT DATA

所在地	フランス、パリ
デザイン・工期	1971-1977年／1996-2000年

Location	Paris, France
Design and Construction	1971-1977／1996-2000

［上］ポンピドー・センター　［下］ポンピドー・センターのファサード　改装後　　*Top* : Centre Georges Pompidou　　*Bottom* : Centre Georges Pompidou façade after renovation

ポンピドー・センター　Centre Georges Pompidou

［左］エスカレーター　［右上］ファサードの一部　青いパイプは空気用ダクト　［右下］ファサードの一部　緑色のパイプは水用ダクト、赤はエレベーター、黄色は電気系統
Left : Escalators　*Top right (upper)* : Detail of façade. Blue pipes are air ducts
Top right (lower) : Detail of façade. Green pipes are water ducts, red indicates elevators, and yellow indicates electrical conduits.

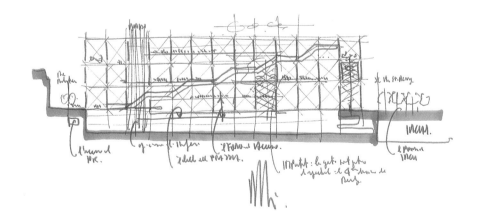

レンゾ・ピアノのスケッチ　Renzo Piano sketch

IBMトラベリング・パビリオン
IBM Traveling Pavilion

IBM社による未来のコンピュータ技術をテーマとした展示のためのパビリオン。移動式というコンセプトを実現すべく、RPBWは展示空間を開発した。展示は1983年から1986年にかけてヨーロッパ20カ所を巡回し、150万人の動員を集めた。パビリオンは、長さ48m、幅12m、高さ6mのトンネル状で、組み立てと解体、輸送を容易にするため均一部材によるモデュール式である。自重耐力性を有するビーチ材とポリカーボネートによる34体の部材が連なって全体を構成。各々の部材は3組のアーチと12のピラミッドが連なった立体的なトラスから成る。その他、アルミニウム製ダイキャストや特殊接着剤等、当時の最先端技術を活用し耐候性が確保された。必要な設備には電力が供給されるよう、またパビリオンを建てた際、設備が風雨にさらされないよう設計され、内部の温湿度は一定に保たれる。

This pavilion was created for IBM to present exhibitions on the theme of future computer technologies. RPBW developed an exhibition space appropriate for realizing the concept for a traveling building. The facility operated from 1983 to 1986, touring twenty locations in Europe, and being seen by 1.5 million people. The pavilion took the form of a 48m long, 12m wide, and 6m tall tunnel vault, using a modular structure with uniform structural members for ease of assembly, disassembly, and transportation. A total of thirty-four self-supporting segments constructed from beech and polycarbonate were linked together, each consisting of three sets of arches and twelve pyramids connected together to produce a three-dimensional lattice truss structure. State-of-the-art technologies ensured weather-proofing, including diecast aluminum elements and special adhesives. The design ensured power supplies for all the equipment in the pavilion, and protected the equipment from the weather during assembly. The pavilion was also able to maintain a steady internal temperature.

レンゾ・ピアノはこのプロジェクトで古いものと新しいものを混合した「新しいカクテル」を作ってみようと考えたという。パリのIBM本社で、会議中に素材の耐久性に疑問が呈された際、レンゾ・ピアノはハンマーをかざしてピラミッドに怒りを込めて強い一撃を加え大音響が鳴り響いたが、引っかき傷すらつかず、プロジェクトは承認された。巡回都市は、ロンドン、リヨン、ヨーク、ローマ、ミラノなど。

Renzo Piano apparently decided to construct this project as a "new cocktail" that mixed the old and the new. When questioned about the durability of the materials during a meeting at IBM in Paris, he produced a hammer and vigorously took out his frustration on one of the pyramids. The noise was impressive but the material remained unscratched, resulting in the project being approved. Venues of the tour were London, Lyon, York, Rome, and Milan, etc.

アムステルダムのフォンデル公園にて
In Vondelpark, Amsterdam

PROJECT DATA

巡回地	ヨーロッパ20都市
デザイン・巡回期間	1982–1986年

Venue	Twenty cities in Europe
Design and the tour	1982–1986

［上］ミラノにて　［下］ヨークにて　*Top* : In Milan　*Bottom* : In York

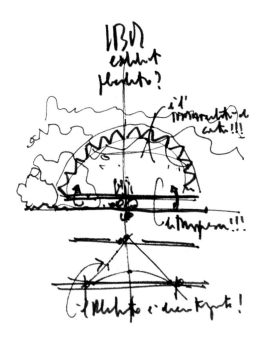

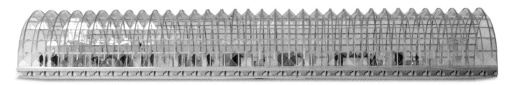

［上］レンゾ・ピアノのスケッチ　［中］全体模型 1:50（1983年）　［下］パリにて　［右ページ］ピラミッド型の立体的な構造体のクローズアップ（ヨークにて）
Top : Renzo Piano sketch　*Middle* : Overall model 1:50 (1983)　*Bottom* : In Paris
Right page : Close up of three dimensional pyramid structure (in York)

チバウ文化センター
Jean-Marie Tjibaou Cultural Center

チバウ文化センターは、ティナ半島の岬の先端に建設された10体から成る小屋群の文化施設である。地元カナック族の文化を紹介、活性化する目的で設立された。暗殺されたニューカレドニアの政治的指導者、ジャン・マリー・チバウを記念して建てられたため、その名前が冠してある。民族の深い自然とのつながりからインスピレーションを得て、民族固有の小屋の形態に倣いつつ、ガラスやアルミニウムなどの現代的な建築材を伝統的な木や石と組み合わせている。土着文化、歴史への理解は、このプロジェクトにおいて最も重要な点だった。小屋は20〜28mの高さがあり、展示スペース、会議室と図書室、絵画や彫刻のスタジオの三つの用途に分かれている。2層のファサードはスリットとルーバーで制御しながら風を取り入れ自然換気を可能にしている。

The Jean-Marie Tjibaou Cultural Center is a cultural complex consisting of ten huts arranged in clusters at the tip of the Tina Peninsula, a spit of land in New Caledonia. It was constructed with the objective of introducing the local Kanak culture and drawing on its traditions, and it honors Jean-Marie Tjibaou, the assassinated New Caledonian political leader whose name it bears. Taking inspiration from the Kanak people's deep ties with nature, the forms of its buildings reference traditional Kanak constructions, combining modern materials such as glass and aluminum with the more traditional wood and stone. Gaining an understanding of Kanak culture and becoming familiar with Kanak history was the most vital part of this project. The "huts" range from 20 to 28m in height, and are grouped according to their functions, which include exhibition spaces, a conference room and library, and studios for painting and sculpture. Double outer façades facilitate passive ventilation, using slits and adjustable louvers to allow light winds to filter through.

レンゾ・ピアノは、ヨーロッパ文化圏と全く異なるこの太平洋文化圏でのプロジェクトをたとえてスープの調理法だけでなく材料そのものも違う場所に、我が家の食器を持たず得意分野だけ携えて乗り込んだと語る。競技設計当初から文化人類学者の協力を得てプロジェクトは進められ、サンゴ、樹皮など土着の素材と現代のアルミやスチール、ガラスなどの建築部材が劇的融合を遂げた。

Explaining his stance for this project in a Pacific Island culture, Renzo Piano said, "When we say 'culture' we usually mean our own: a fine soup blended from [European influences]. In the Pacific it is not just the recipe that is different but the ingredients as well. ... I didn't bring my own cutlery. All I brought were my skills and those of the Building Workshop..." Seeking the cooperation of cultural anthropologists from the design competition stage led to achieving a dramatic fusion of indigenous materials, such as coral and tree bark, with modern construction materials, such as aluminum, steel, and glass.

ティナ半島岬の先端に位置する「カーズ」の一群
Cluster of New Caledonian huts at the tip of the Tina Peninsula

PROJECT DATA

所在地	ニューカレドニア、ヌーメア
デザイン・工期	1991-1998年

Location	Nouméa, New Caledonia
Design and Construction	1991-1998

チバウ文化センター　Jean-Marie Tjibaou Cultural Center

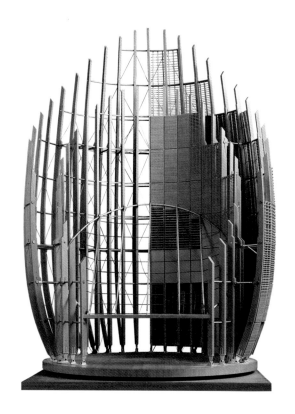

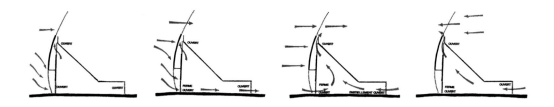

［上］、［中］「カーズ」の発展－試作模型　1:20　［下］自然換気の空気の流れを示す図
Top, Middle : Hut development: Experimental model 1:20　*Bottom* : Diagrams of air flow for natural ventilation

［上］ファサードのスリットと構造体　　［下］チバウ文化センター
Top : Façade slits and structure　　*Bottom* : Jean-Marie Tjibaou Cultural Center

ザ・シャード
The Shard - London Bridge Tower

「シャード」とは「ガラスの破片」の意味で、本作が8断面のガラスを組み合わせた72層建て地上309.6mのタワーであることから。徐々に空の中に消えていくような幻惑的な効果を狙って設計された塔の最上部240mの位置に、スカイラインの遊歩道と展望台がある。8断面の間には空隙があり、予想しえない光の反射を生じさせる視覚的側面とともに自然換気を可能にしている。上に行くほど細くなるこの塔は、そのフロア面積に応じて様々な施設を収容しており、下層にはオフィスや公共施設、レストラン、中層にはホテル、上層は高層マンションである。ロンドンブリッジ駅周辺をさらに発展させ公共交通機関の利便性を高め自動車交通の渋滞を減じるというロンドン市長の方針に沿い、駅周辺の再開発と再統合につながったプロジェクトである。

The shape of the Shard is defined by eight glass facades that resemble shards, the slivers of glass that give the tower its name. Rising to a height of 309.6m, it encompasses seventy-two stories and was designed to produce the mesmerizing effect of tapering off and disappearing into the sky. The highest stories include an open air sky deck and public viewing gallery 240m above the ground. Gaps between the eight shards produce unexpected reflections of light, fulfilling a visual function as well as providing a means of natural ventilation. The tapered shape reduces the floor area of successive stories, which accommodate different functions in accordance with their size. Offices, public spaces, and restaurants occupy the lower floors, a hotel takes up the middle, and there are private apartments at the top. In line with the mayor of London's policy of encouraging redevelopment around London Bridge Station to enhance public transport and reduce traffic congestion, this project incorporated redevelopment of part of the station concourse and is associated with regeneration of the surroundings.

レンゾ・ピアノにヨーロッパで最も高い高層ビル建設の話を持ちかけたのは、ロンドンの60年代のスインギング・ロンドンで有名なカーナビー・ストリートにファッション店舗をもっていて、後に不動産業者に転じたアーヴィング・セラーである。2000年5月セラーとロンドンで会った時、ピアノはまさかこんな冒険に連れて行かれる話だとは思っていなかったと語り、もしザ・シャードの物語を始めるならここから始めるだろうと述べている。

It was Irvine Sellar, who owned a fashion boutique on the famous Carnaby Street in the Swinging London of the 1960s and later became a property developer, who first discussed with Renzo Piano the idea of constructing Europe's tallest skyscraper. Piano explains that when he met with Sellar in London in May 2000, he had no idea that the discussion would lead to such an undertaking, but that meeting should be the starting point for any story about the Shard.

ザ・シャードとロンドンの街
The Shard and London cityscape

PROJECT DATA

所在地	イギリス、ロンドン
デザイン・工期	2000-2012年

Location	London, UK
Design and Construction	2000-2012

セント・ポール大聖堂からザ・シャードを見る　The Shard viewed from St Paul's Cathedral

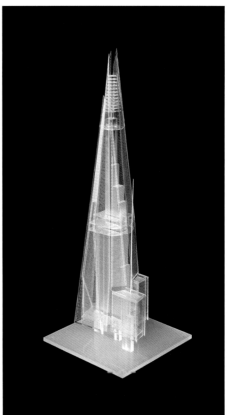

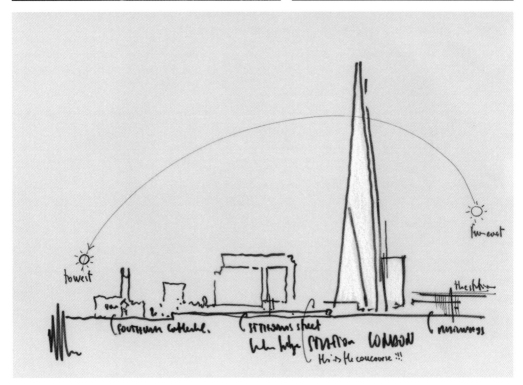

［左ページ］霧の中にかすんで消えるザ・シャード最上部
［上左］夕暮れ時のザ・シャード
［上右］ザ・シャードの模型　1:500
［下］レンゾ・ピアノのスケッチ

Left page : Tip of the Shard fading into the mist
Top left : The Shard at dusk
Top right : Model of the Shard 1:500
Bottom : Renzo Piano sketch

ジェローム・セドゥ・パテ財団
Jérôme Seydoux Pathé Foundation

パリ13区に建てられたマルチ・シネマで有名なジェローム・セドゥ・パテ財団の新本部で映画アーカイブを有する展示上映施設。もともと19世紀半ばには劇場があり、20世紀になって映画館となった建物である。ゴベリン通りに面したファサードには若き日のオーギュスト・ロダンの彫刻もある。RPBWはこうした歴史ある建物や景観を保存しつつ、地区の建築規制により適合する建築計画を立てた。内側の2棟を壊して空いた敷地に、ガラス壁で覆われた「温室」のような建物と「生き物」のような曲がりくねった銀色の量塊状の建物、緑溢れる中庭の複合体を作ったのである。「生き物」は通りからちらっと見える程度で昼間は控えめだが、夜になるとにぶく光って存在感を増す。この甲羅状の屋根は7千枚のアルミニウム製ブラインドで日照に応じて可動し、晴れた日には室内に自然光が溢れる。

This is the new headquarters building and archive screening facility built in the XIII arrondissement of Paris for the Jérôme Seydoux Pathé Foundation, which is named after Jérôme Seydoux, who led the multiplex revolution in France. Pathé opened a cinema on this site in the twentieth century, taking over the building from a mid-nineteenth century theater. The façade on the avenue des Gobelins incorporates sculptures by a young Auguste Rodin. RPBW preserved this historic façade and streetscape, inserting a new architecture compliant with building restrictions in the Gobelins area. Behind the façade, two buildings were demolished to open up the space, replacing them with a complex that combines a glass-covered greenhouse-like structure and the curving silver volume of an organic-shaped "creature," along with a courtyard with trees and flowers. The "creature" can only be glimpsed from the street, and is a discreet presence during the day. At night, it asserts itself with a soft glow. The shell-like roof employs some 7,000 aluminum blinds that can be moved in response to sunlight. On fine days, the interior is bathed in natural light.

当初アルマジロや鯨、熱気球のような形の有機的な、何かが溢れ出るような形態、というアイデアが浮かんだ時の気持ちを、レンゾ・ピアノはノアの箱舟で航海に出たようだったと語っている。中庭には背の高いバーチの木の植栽もされ、生き物のような建築本体と相まって都市の中に小宇宙のような異世界が誕生した。19世紀にはゴベリン劇場、1934年にロダン映画館となった場所である。地下にある66席の映写劇場では、ピアノ演奏で貴重な無声映画が上映されている。

Renzo Piano describes the feeling he experienced when striking upon the idea of an organic form brimming forth with something—like the shape of an armadillo, whale, or a hot-air balloon—as being like embarking on a voyage on Noah's ark. Tall birches planted in the courtyard combined with the creature-like architecture itself to create an otherworldly place like a microcosm within the city. The site had been the location for the Théâtre des Gobelins in the nineteenth century, and the Gaumont Gobelins-Rodin cinema in 1934. Precious silent films from the archives are shown in the 66-seat underground screening room, with a piano accompaniment to the film projected on the screen.

ゴベリン通りから見た建物
Building seen from Avenue des Gobelins

PROJECT DATA

所在地	フランス、パリ
デザイン・工期	2006-2014年

Location	Paris, France
Design and Construction	2006-2014

中庭から見た甲羅状の屋根（2014年）　Carapace-like roof seen from the courtyard

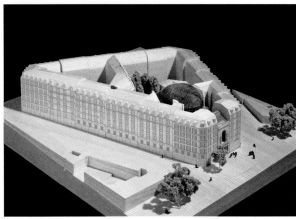

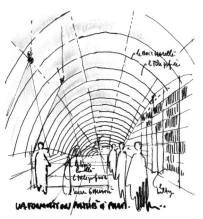

［左ページ］ゴベリン通りの別の建物の屋上から見た敷地全体の様子
［上］5層目の内部の様子　集成木材による構造体
［下左］ジェローム・セドゥ・パテ財団の模型　1:200
［下右］レンゾ・ピアノのスケッチ

Left page : Overall view of site from another building on the Avenue des Gobelins
Top : Inside the building on the 5th level, showing the cross laminated wood structure
Bottom left : Jérôme Seydoux Pathé Foundation model 1:200
Bottom right : Renzo Piano sketch

アカデミー映画博物館
Academy Museum of Motion Pictures

ロサンゼルス中心部、著名なミラクル・マイル地区に建設されたアカデミー映画博物館である。1939年に竣工したメイ・カンパニー・デパートのビル、以後サバン・ビルと名前を変えた流線型デザインの歴史的なビルを保存修復しつつ、その脇に、1946年に遡ることのできるビルを新たに球体のビルとして移設新設した。この全体計画にRPBWが携わった。球体のビルには、客席数千席の「デイヴィット・ゲフィン劇場」と「ドルビー・ファミリー・テラス」という展望テラスがある。このテラスは、透明なボールのような球体の形状をしたビルの上層部にあり、半球形のガラスとスチールの庇で覆われて光と風の溢れる空間である。ここからかの有名なハリウッドサインのある山々が連なる景観を見渡すことができる。2021年に開館。

The Academy Museum of Motion Pictures is situated on the Miracle Mile in the heart of Los Angeles. It preserves the historic Saban Building, an example of Streamline Moderne style completed in 1939 as the May Company department store building. Alongside it, the project replaced 1946 additions with a new spherical building. RPBW was involved in the whole project, including the spherical building's 1,000-seat David Geffen Theater and Dolby Family Terrace. The terrace tops what looks like a glass sphere, and is covered by a domed glass and steel canopy, producing a light and airy space. Views include the range of hills with the famous Hollywood Sign. The facility opened in 2021.

レンゾ・ピアノがこれまでに影響を受けた建築家として挙げているのが、構造家のルイージ・ネルヴィやバックミンスター・フラーである。後者は移設可能なジオデシック・ドームの発明で知られるアメリカの建築家。ピアノは、現代の技術に即した独自の構造体による恒久的な建築物として、軽量で太陽熱エネルギーを循環させるシステムとしての透明なドームを実現している。

Renzo Piano lists structural engineer Pier Luigi Nervi and R. Buckminster Fuller as architects who have influenced his work. Fuller was an American architect known for inventing the portable geodesic dome. For the Academy Museum of Motion Pictures, Piano created a lightweight, transparent dome with a novel structure based on current technology to serve as a system for circulating solar thermal energy in a permanent building.

ドルビー・ファミリー・テラス
Dolby Family Terrace

PROJECT DATA

所在地	アメリカ、ロサンゼルス
デザイン・工期	2012-2020年

Location	Los Angeles, USA
Design and Construction	2000-2012

［上］デイヴィット・ゲフィン劇場のドーム　［下］航空写真　建物と敷地、ロサンゼルスの街　*Top*：David Geffen Theater dome　*Bottom*：Aerial photo of buildings and site in Los Angeles

アカデミー映画博物館　全体写真　Academy Museum of Motion Pictures overall

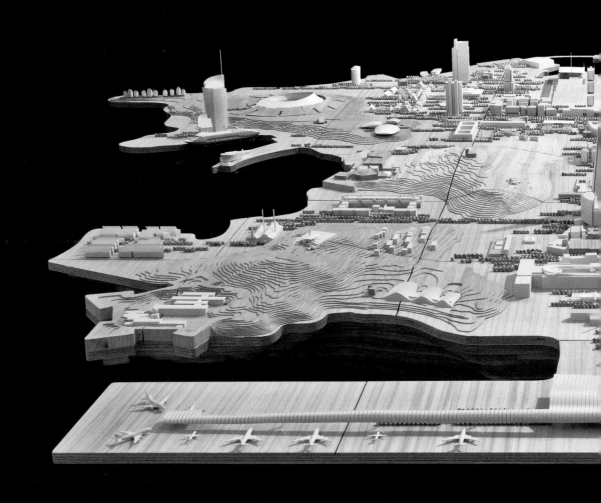

レンゾ・ピアノ「アトランティス島」（2018年）

レンゾ・ピアノの活動初期から現在進行中のプロジェクトまで、全102の建築作品をひとつの架空の島に落とし込んだ壮大な模型が、この「アトランティス島」である。プラトンの著作に登場するジブラルタル海峡の外側にあったとされる伝説の島およびそこに繁栄した帝国「アトランティス」に因んで名付けられた。1番目は1969年ジェノヴァに建てられた最初のレンゾ・ピアノ事務所で102番目はリスボンに今後完成する予定の集合住宅。全世界で建造されてきたピアノの半世紀にわたる建築作品が一堂に集まった夢の島である。

Renzo Piano, *Atlantis* (2018)

This magnificent imaginary island incorporates scale models of all 102 of Renzo Piano's built works, from his earliest days to the projects underway at the point the model was produced. It is named for Atlantis, the mythical island with a flourishing empire described by Plato as lying beyond the straits of Gibraltar. Building number 1 is the first Renzo Piano office constructed in Genoa in 1969, and building number 102 is a residential complex in Lisbon that has yet to be completed. This marvelous island brings together all the architectural works built by Piano throughout the world in a single place.

「アトランティス島」の地図
Map of *Atlantis*

島には102の建築模型が配置されている。緑色の印があるのが本書で紹介しているレンゾ・ピアノの建築作品。新宮晋とのコラボレーション（コラボレーション5を除く）にはオレンジの印を併記した。

The island contains 102 architectural models. Those with a green marker are the architectural works of Renzo Piano described in this book. His collaborations with Susumu Shingu (apart from collaboration 5) also have an orange marker.

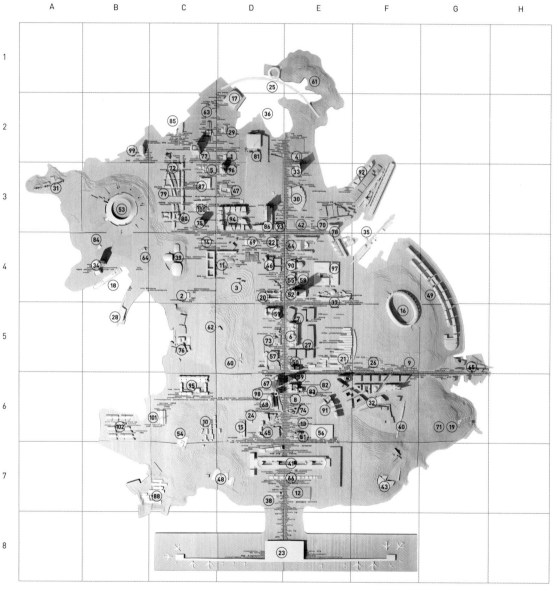

建築模型（全て同じスケール 1:1000）　architectural models (all same scale 1:1000)

RPBW（パリ）にて　2018年　at RPBW Paris in 2018

新宮 晋 ＋ レンゾ・ピアノ
年表

Susumu Shingu + Renzo Piano
Chronology

新日本建設
初三 新宮 晋

習字も習っていた
Also learns calligraphy.

新宮 晋
Susumu Shingu

7月13日、日本・大阪に誕生

Born in Osaka, Japan on July 13.

《大阪駅》(1948年)
Osaka Station (1948)

《障子張》(1949年)
Shoujibari (1949)

《中之島公会堂》(1953年)
Nakanoshima Public Hall (1953)

男ばかりの4人兄弟の末っ子として、大阪・豊中に生まれる
商社勤めの父は、海外勤務が長く、和洋折衷な雰囲気な家庭に育つ

Born in Toyonaka City, Osaka Prefecture as the youngest of four brothers.
With his father working for a trading company and spending a lot of time traveling abroad, Shingu is raised in a household with an atmosphere that is a blend of Japanese and Western lifestyles.

家族写真、豊中 (1942年)
His family in Toyonaka (1942)

物心のついた時から絵を描くのが大好きで、あだ名は「絵描き」。
祖母からの提案で親戚の画家・小磯良平に絵をみてもらうことになる。
小学生の頃には絵画コンクールでたびたび入賞

As a child, loves drawing, from as far back as he remembers. Acquires the nickname 'Ekaki' (artist). Is tutored in art by a relative, the painter Ryohei Koiso, at the suggestion of his grandmother. Frequently wins awards in art competitions in elementary school.

1937 [0歳 (age)]

1937~ [幼少期～青年期 (childhood～adolescence)]

1937~ [幼少期～青年期 (childhood～adolescence)]

9月14日、イタリア・ジェノヴァに誕生

Born in Genoa, Italy on September 14.

レンゾ・ピアノ
Renzo Piano

5歳のレンゾ・ピアノ
Renzo Piano aged five

3人兄弟 (兄・妹) の第二子として、ジェノヴァで建設業を営む一家に生まれる

Born in Genoa, Italy into a family of builders, with an elder brother and younger sister.

父、兄と私の間には建築に寄せる情熱から生じた特別なきずながあった
母や妹との愛情のきずなもまた、極めて強いものだった

Passion for architecture created a special bond between me, my father, and my brother.
And there was a very strong bond of love with my mother and sister, too.

幼い頃から、父親のカルロを追って建設現場へ。
現場の職人たちの仕事に魅了された

From childhood, accompanied his father Carlo to building construction sites.
Impressed by the artisans.

建設現場でのピアノの父、カルロ・ピアノ　建設現場にて (1960年代)
Renzo's father Carlo Piano on site (1960s)

東京藝術大学
絵画科に入学

Enters Tokyo
National University of
Fine Arts and Music
(now Tokyo University
of the Arts),
where he studies
oil painting.

東京藝大1年、下宿にて
Tokyo University of the Arts 1st year,
at boarding house

《オペラ》(1966年)
Opera (1966)

《植物の交信》(1968年)
Communication of Plants (1968)

帰国後、大阪の造船所の
援助を受けながら、
風で動く彫刻を制作

After returning to Japan,
creates sculptural works
that move with the wind with
support from a shipbuilding
company in Osaka.

とうとうぼくは、世界中の誰もやっていない、独自の世界を発見した。
I finally discover a distinctive world that no one else on earth is engaging in.

1960年からイタリア政府の
奨学生としてローマへ留学

滞在する6年間で手がけるものが
具象画から抽象画、立体へと変化し、
動く立体作品を作り始める

[右写真] イタリア、ピサにて (1962年頃)
Right : In Pisa, Italy (C.1962)

Studies in Rome on a scholarship from the Italian government starting in
1960. Shifts his focus during his six years in Italy from representational
painting to abstract painting, and then to three-dimensional art, and
begins to create three-dimensional works that move.

1967年9月、日比谷公園で
初めての野外彫刻展「風の造形」展を開催

Holds his first outdoor sculpture exhibition
Wind Structures in Hibiya Park in September 1967.

「風の造形」展、日比谷公園 (1967年)
"Wind Structures" in Hibiya Park (1967)

1956〜 [19歳(age)〜]

1958〜 [21歳(age)〜]

ル・コルビュジエ「ユニテ・ダビタシオン」「マルセイユ、フランス」にて (1958年)
At Le Corbusier's Unité d'Habitation in Marseille, France (1958)

1958年よりフィレンツェ大学に2年通学

この後、1960年9月からフランコ・アルビーニの
スタジオで働く。12月にミラノ工科大学に入学 (-1964年)。
1965年、パリに赴き、ジャン・プルーヴェと出会い、
プレハブ建築をはじめ、彼から多くを学ぶ

Studied at the University of Florence for two years
from 1958, then worked at the office of Franco Albini
from September 1960.
Entered the Politecnico of Milan University
in December, graduating in 1964.
Subsequently worked mainly in Milan,
but often visiting London. In 1965, moved to Paris,
where he met and learned about prefabricated
architecture and much more from Jean Prouvé.

スタジオ・ピアノ (1968-1969年、イタリア、ジェノヴァ)
Studio Piano Office, 1968-1969, Genoa, Italy

1968年に建てられた最初のレンゾ・ピアノの
オフィス。窓のない20m四方の壁で囲まれた
自由配置空間で、天井から採光を行う構造体だった

Renzo Piano's first office,
constructed in 1968.
Windowless walls surrounded
an open-plan space on a 20m-square base,
with natural light illumination from the ceiling.

スタジオ・レンゾ・ピアノ (イタリア、ジェノヴァ、エルゼッリ)
Studio Piano, Erzelli, Genoa, Italy

1967 研究モデル
1967 Research model

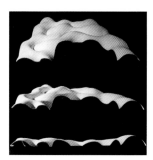

第14回ミラノ・トリエンナーレで発表された
シェル構造システム
Shell structural system for the 14th
Milan Triennale

1965-1969年の間にモデュラー方式の
壁やポリエチレン製膜構造の屋根等で
5つの特許を取得

1965-1969, acquired five patents
relating to modular walls and
polyester membrane structures.

スプーンに溜まった水が傾いてこぼれると、
反対側に吊るされたコーン型の重しが水面を叩いて音を出す。
6つの異なる音がランダムに奏でるエンドレス・ミュージック

When a spoon full of water tips over and spills, a cone-shaped weight hanging
from the opposite end hits the surface of the water, creating a sound.
"Endless music" is produced in which six different sounds are created randomly.

《フローティング・サウンド》（1970年） *Floating Sound* (1970)

造船技術を生かした作品《フローティング・サウンド》を
70年大阪万博の人工池「進歩の湖」に浮かべる

Floats the work *Floating Sound*, which incorporates ship building technology,
on the artificial pond Lake of Progress at Expo '70 Osaka.

《フローティング・サウンド》スケッチ（1970年）
Floating Sound, sketch (1970)

1970~ ［33歳(age)~］

1970~ ［33歳(age)~］

大阪万博イタリア産業館

（1969-1970年、日本、大阪）

Pavilion of Italian Industry,
Osaka World's Fair, 1969-1970, Osaka, Japan

強化ポリエステルと堅牢な鉄骨による軽量性、
輸送性、耐久性にすぐれたグリッド・システムによる
パビリオン。イタリア館にはこのとき二つの
パビリオンがあり、その内のひとつだった

Pavilion design with reinforced polyester
within a steel structure, using a grid system
to achieve lightness, transportability, and durability.
Constructed alongside the Italian national pavilion.

マレ地区の歴史的建造物の街並みとポンピドー・センター Centre Georges Pompidou in the historical townscape of the Marais

ポンピドー・センター （1971-1977年）

Centre Georges Pompidou

パリ中心部の歴史的建造物が立ち並ぶマレ地区に位置する文化センター。
その前衛性が世界を震撼させた

Cultural Center situated in the Marais amid the dense urban fabric of old Paris.
Radical design shook the world.

ポンピドー・センターは人生の学校であり、冒険の発見にほかならなかった。
その後も続く冒険の仲間の多くを、私はその時に得た

Through the Pompidou Centre project, I learned about life and
discovered adventure. Most of my partners in subsequent adventures were
people I first worked with during this period.

1973 帆船図面
Sailing Boat, Didon

レンゾ・ピアノによる
ヨットのデザイン
Yacht design
by Renzo Piano

雑創の森（1977年）　Zasso Forest School (1977)

京都府にある「雑創の森学園」の建設プロジェクトに参加。
7つの塔と7体の風見を制作。
79年に第4回吉田五十八賞を受賞

Participates in a construction project for Zasso no Morigakuen
Soyokaze Kindergarten in Kyoto Prefecture.
Creates seven towers and seven weathervanes.
Wins the 4th Yoshida Isoya Prize in 1979.

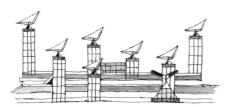

雑創の森　スケッチ（1977年）
Zasso Forest School, sketch (1977)

雑創の森　風車（1977年）
Zasso Forest School, Windmill (1977)

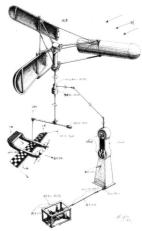

雑創の森　デッサン（1977年）
Zasso Forest School, drawing (1977)

クライアント・建築家・アーティスト皆が30代。一緒に考え、一緒に作り出した

The clients, architects, and artists are all in their thirties.
They all come up with ideas together and create together.

1975〜 [38歳(age)〜]

1981〜 [44歳(age)〜]

メニル・コレクション美術館 （1981-1987年、アメリカ、ヒューストン）
Museum for the Menil Collection

ドメニク・ド・メニル夫人による1万点もの美術コレクションを
展示した美術館。「リーフ」と名付けられた同一形態の反復による
モデュール式の屋根が特徴的である

Museum to house and exhibit Dominique and
John de Menil's collection of more than 10,000 works of art.
Features a modular roof structure filtering zenithal natural light
through a series of "Leaves."

IBMトラベリング・パビリオン （1982-1986年）
IBM Traveling Pavilion

IBM社による未来のコンピュータ技術をテーマとした
展示のためのパビリオン。
モデュール式の構造体を特徴とする。
ヨーロッパ20カ所を巡回し、150万人の動員を集めた

Modular structure pavilion for
an IBM exhibition on advances
in computer technology.
Touring twenty destinations in Europe,
the exhibition was seen by 1.5 million people.

アートとは何か？　僕のやっていることが本当にアートなのか？
What is art? Are my own creations really art?

Windcircus

10点の風で動く彫刻を40フィートのコンテナ一本に詰めて旅に出た。
「ウインドサーカス」は、ヨーロッパ、アメリカの全9都市を巡回

Goes on the road with a 40-foot-long container holding ten sculptures that move with the wind. Windcircus exhibition tours nine cities in Europe and America.

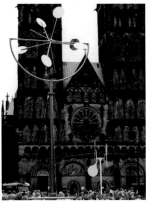
ドイツ、ブレーメン
Bremen, Germany

[上] スペイン、バルセロナ
[下] フィンランド、ラハティ
Top : Barcelona, Spain
Bottom : Lahti, Finland

アメリカ、ロサンゼルス
Los Angeles, USA

[上] アメリカ、ニューヨーク
[下] アメリカ、シカゴ
Top : New York, USA
Bottom : Chicago, USA

1987〜　[50歳(age)〜]

1987〜　[50歳(age)〜]

夜のスタジアム外観
Stadium from outside at night

スタジアム内
Inside the stadium

サン・ニコラ・サッカー・スタジアム（1987-1990年、イタリア、バーリ）
San Nicola Football Stadium

イタリア、プーリア地方の町、バーリに1990年ワールド・カップ開催の年に完成したサッカー場。6万人収容可能

Football stadium completed in Bari in the Apulia region of Italy in time for the 1990 World Cup. Capacity of nearly 60,000 seats.

バイエラー財団美術館（1991-1997年、スイス、リーエン[バーゼル]）
Museum for the Beyeler Foundation

モダン・アートのコレクターであるエルンスト・バイエラーのコレクションを展示するための美術館として建設

Constructed as an art museum dedicated to exhibiting the collection of modern art assembled by Ernst Beyeler.

チバウ文化センター（1991-1998年）
Jean-Marie Tjibaou Cultural Center

ティナ半島の岬の先端に建設された10体から成る小屋群の文化施設。地元カナック族の文化を紹介、活性化する目的で設立された

Cultural complex consisting of ten huts arranged in clusters at the tip of the Tina Peninsula. Constructed to introduce the local Kanak culture and draw on its traditions.

《コロンブスの風》（1992年） *Columbus's Wind (1992)*

《はてしない空》（1994年） *Boundless Sky (1994)*

不可能なものは何もない
Nothing is impossible

────── ピーター・ライス Peter Rice

見えない空気の流れを見えるようにしてくれないか？
Can you make the streams of air visible？

────── レンゾ・ピアノ Renzo Piano

01 │ コラボレーション Collaborations

ジェノヴァ港再開発 ＋ コロンブスの風
Re-development of the Genoa Old Harbour ＋ Columbus's Wind

■ **1992** ［55歳(age)］

レンゾ・ピアノによるコロンブス新大陸発見500年記念万博に際して行われたカリカメント広場に隣接したジェノヴァ旧港の再開発。来訪者が港岸エリアを楽しめるようになって現在に至っている。旧港の建造物の修復とともに、万博のシンボルとなった「ビゴ」とフェスティヴァル会場、水族館が新設。ともに、新宮晋の彫刻が実現した。

Renzo Piano's redevelopment of Genoa's old harbor adjacent to Piazza Caricamento took place at the time of the International Exhibition Genoa '92 – Colombo '92 (Columbus International Exposition) celebrating 500 years since Columbus discovered America. It allowed people to visit the port to enjoy the area along the waterside, an advantage that continues to this day. In addition to restoring buildings in the old harbor, the project created the Bigo, a symbol of the expo, as well as the Piazza delle Feste (festival plaza) and an aquarium. It also incorporates sculpture by Susumu Shingu.

デザイン・工期 (Design and Construction)：1985–2001

02 │ コラボレーション Collaborations

関西国際空港旅客ターミナルビル ＋ はてしない空
Kansai International Airport Passenger Terminal Building ＋ Boundless Sky

■ **1994** ［57歳(age)］

大阪湾に新設された飛行場で、1988年国際設計競技によりRPBWが設計者に決定。1994年に開港。全体はグライダーが島の上に休んでいるかのような形状で、横に拡がる翼の両端幅は1.7kmにも及ぶ。最上階にある国際線出発フロアの波型の屋根の形態は空気の拡散の流れの研究成果に基づくもの。この天井から新宮晋の彫刻が吊ってある。

RPBW became the designer for the passenger terminal of a new airport to be constructed in Osaka Bay through an international design competition held in 1988. The overall shape of the terminal building of the airport, which opened in 1994, resembles a glider resting on the island, with the wings extending outwards on both sides, measuring 1.7km from tip to tip. The roof of the uppermost level, international departures, has a wave-like shape based on studies of the distribution of airflow. Sculptures by Susumu Shingu are affixed to the ceiling.

デザイン・工期 (Design and Construction)：1988–1994

ジェノヴァ港 Genoa Old Harbour

人工島全体の航空写真（1994年） Aerial photo of the Airport Island (1994)

キッピスと仲間たち（1994年）　*"Kippis and His Friends"* (1994)

三田市青野ダムサイト公園の彫刻
《水の木》完成を祝って、企画・演出を手掛けた
野外劇「キッピスと仲間たち」を上演

The outdoor performance *"Kippis and His Friends"*
planned and directed by Shingu, is held in celebration of
the completion of the sculpture *Water Tree*
in Aono Dam Park, Sanda City.

1994〜 [57歳(age)〜]

1992〜 [55歳(age)〜]

デビス・ビル C1
Debis Headquarters C1

劇場とデビス・ビル D1+C1
Theater and Debis D1 + C1

ポツダム広場再開発計画（1992-2000年、ドイツ、ベルリン）
Reconstruction of Potsdamer Platz

1989年のベルリンの壁崩壊後、RPBWは1992年に行われた
ポツダム広場再生の全体計画のコンペで勝者となり、
劇場やオフィスビル、IMAXやホールを設計した。
同時に全体計画内の他の施設の設計にコンペに参加した
数人の建築家を招聘した。

After the fall of the Berlin Wall in 1989,
RPBW won the competition for a masterplan
Renovate Potsdamer Platz in 1992.
RPBW invited other architects who had worked on the
competition to design several buildings, while RPBW
designed the theater, office buildings,
IMAX and the auditorium.

《雨の軌跡》（1995年）　*Locus of Rain* (1995)

この《雨の軌跡》にはレオナルドがいる
Trace of Leonardo in *Locus of Rain*

——————　マーティン・ケンプ Martin Kemp

03 ｜ コラボレーション　Collaborations

リンゴット工場再開発計画 ＋ 雨の軌跡
Lingotto Factory Conversion ＋ Locus of Rain

■ 1995 [58歳(age)]

建築史上重要な近代建築であり自動車工場であるトリノにある「リン
ゴット・ファクトリー」は、1920年代の鉄筋コンクリートによる先進的な
建築で、5層立てのビルの屋上に自動車のテスト走行のためのサーキット
があることで知られる。1982年に閉鎖された後、フィアット社は設計競技
を行い、RPBWが翌年勝者となってこの建築の改装を実施。

The Lingotto Factory, a car manufacturing plant in Turin,
Italy, is historically significant as a prime example of
modernist architecture. It was an advanced building in the
1920s, built with reinforced concrete, and famous for having
a track for testing automobiles on the rooftop of the
five-story building. After the factory closed in 1982, Fiat
S.p.A. held a design competition, which RPBW won the
following year, giving it the contract to convert the building.

デザイン・工期 (Design and Construction)：1983-2003

ジョヴァンニ ＋ マレッラ・アニェッリ・ピクチャー・ギャラリー
Giovanni and Marella Agnelli Picture Gallery

《海の響き》（1995年） *Resonance of the Sea* (1995)

ウェルカム・アート
Welcome art

────── 新宮晋 Susumu Shingu

04 ｜ コラボレーション　Collaborations

レンゾ・ピアノ・ビルディング・ワークショップ ＋ 海の響き
Renzo Piano Building Workshop ＋ Resonance of the Sea

■ 1995 ［58歳（age）］

リグリア海に面した段丘の斜面にあるRPBWのジェノヴァ本部の建物。建物の全体は土地と同じ段状の構造で、リヴィエラ地方に典型的な温室の形状を想起させるものである。事務所内にも植栽され、緑と光と海に溢れた内と外の境界線のない環境が生み出された。建物からガラス越しに見える海に面した緑の斜面に、新宮晋の彫刻がある。

The Genoa headquarters of the Renzo Piano Building Workshop sits perched on the slopes of the terraced coastline facing the Ligurian Sea. Stepping down the hillside in a series of terraces like the surrounding landscape, the building overall brings to mind the shape of the greenhouses that are typical along the terraced Italian Riviera. Plants are grown inside the structure, creating an environment brimming with greenery, light, and the sea, without boundaries between inside and outside. Sculptures by Susumu Shingu on a green hillside facing the sea can be seen through glass from inside the building.

デザイン・工期（Design and Construction）：1989-1991

太陽光が降り注ぐ事務所内部の様子
Rooms in the workshop catch abundant sunlight.

彩の国さいたま芸術劇場で
「星のあやとり スペース・ファンタジー」を上演。
企画・演出を手がける

"Cat's Cradle of the Stars" is performed at Saitama Arts Theater.
Shingu handles planning and direction.

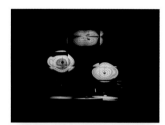

星のあやとり スペース・ファンタジー
"Cat's Cradle of the Stars"

1997〜 ［60歳（age）〜］

1996〜 ［59歳（age）〜］

プリツカー賞受賞
（1998年）

Pritzker Prize winner

ホワイトハウスにて。プリツカー賞受賞時の写真 右がレンゾ・ピアノ、左がジェイ・プリツカー

Receiving the Pritzker Prize at the White House.
Renzo Piano (right) with Jay Pritzker (left)

オーロラ・プレイス
（1996-2000年、
オーストラリア、シドニー）

Aurora Place
Office and Residential
Buildings

航空写真。シドニー・オペラ・ハウスが湾岸にある。
Aerial photo. Sydney Opera House is by the bay

224mのオフィス棟と75mのマンションの複合プロジェクト。2000年シドニー・オリンピックの年にシドニー・オペラハウスや王立植物園のあるポート・ジャクソン湾近くに竣工

Complex with 224m office tower and 75m residential tower. Completed in time for the 2000 Sydney Olympics near Port Jackson, home to the Sydney Opera House and Royal Botanic Gardens.

《雲との対話》(1998年) *Dialogue with Clouds* (1998)

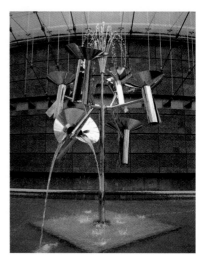

《水の花》(1999年) *Water Flower* (1999)

上を向いて歩こう
Looking up

—— 新宮晋 Susumu Shingu

05 | コラボレーション Collaborations

メリディアーナ・センター ＋ 雲との対話
Meridiana Shopping Center and Offices ＋ Dialogue with Clouds

■ 1998 [61歳(age)]

アルプス山脈に近い町、レッコの中心部に建造されたビル。広い緑地公園に囲まれて、正方形の敷地には、ハイパーマーケットや店舗、2千台収容可能な巨大駐車場がある。湖面のように深い水色のガラスのファサードは、光を反射し輝きながらこの地の四季折々の豊かな自然を映し出す。新宮晋の彫刻はこのビルの最も高い位置に5体ある。

This multipurpose complex in the center of Lecco, a town in northern Lombardy close to the Alps, consists of three independent high-rise towers providing group housing, commercial facilities, and offices, among other things. The deep blue appearance of the glass facades echoes the blue of the lake, reflecting light and the natural beauty of the surroundings as they change around the year. Sculptures by Susumu Shingu are installed at the highest points of the buildings.

デザイン・工期 (Design and Construction) : 1988-1999

ゼロからのスタート
Starting from zero

—— 新宮晋 Susumu Shingu

06 | コラボレーション Collaborations

バンカ・ポポラーレ・ディ・ローディ ＋ 水の花
Banca Popolare di Lodi ＋ Water Flower

■ 1999 [62歳(age)]

ロンバルディア州を代表する銀行、バンカ・ポポラーレ・ディ・ローディ本部のための建築物。伝統的な建築材テラコッタを用いた開かれた建築空間で、軽量ガラスと細いスチール鋼によるキャノピー(天蓋型の庇)に覆われた大広場は建物の内側と外部を繋ぐ空間であり、様々な人々が出会う場でもある。この大広場に新宮晋の彫刻がある。

This project was constructed as the headquarters of the Banca Popolare di Lodi, the leading bank of the Lombardy region. This open and airy architectural space employs terracotta, a traditional building material of the region. The large piazza covered by a canopy made of lightweight glass and thin steel ties connects the inside and outside of the building, serving as a place where various people come together. Sculpture work by Susumu Shingu is located in the piazza.

デザイン・工期 (Design and Construction) : 1991-2001

上空から敷地全域を撮影した写真
Whole site photographed from above

バンカ・ポポラーレ・ディ・ローディ 中庭
Banca Popolare di Lodi, piazza

三宅一生パリ・コレクション（1999春夏）の舞台装置を制作する

Handles stage design for
Issey Miyake Paris Collection spring/summer 1999.

三宅一生1999春夏パリ・コレクション
Issey Miyake Paris Collection spring/summer 1999.

21点の風で動く彫刻を一本のコンテナに詰めて僻地を巡る「ウインドキャラバン」を行った。未来の生き方のヒントを求めて

Holds *Wind Caravan* exhibition,
which travels to remote locations with
a container holding twenty-one sculptures
that move with the wind, in pursuit of ideas
about future lifestyles.

日本、三田　Sanda, Japan

ニュージーランド、モトコレア　Motukorea, New Zealand

フィンランド、イナリ　Inari, Finland

モロッコ、タムダハト　Tamedakhte, Morocco

モンゴル、ウンドルドブ　Undur Dov, Mongolia

ブラジル、クンブーコ　Cumbuco, Brasil

1999～ ［62歳（age）～］

1998～ ［61歳（age）～］

マディソン通りに面した正面入口
Main entrance on Madison Avenue

エントランス・ロビー
Entrance lobby

モルガン・ライブラリー修復拡張プロジェクト
Renovation and Expansion of the Morgan Library
（2000-2006年、アメリカ、ニューヨーク）

銀行家のJ.P.モルガンの35万点のコレクションを収蔵する図書館。
19世紀に建造されたパッラーディオ様式の建物を修復し、
狭い敷地内に地下を深く掘る解決法によってスペースを広げた

Houses the 350,000 volume library of banker J.P. Morgan.
Renovated architecture dating from the nineteenth century, retaining
a Palladian portal and creating space by expanding downward.

ニューヨーク・タイムズ・ビル
The New York Times Building
（2000-2007年、アメリカ、ニューヨーク）

光と反射が絶えず移り変わる「石化した林」と
ピアノが形容する摩天楼の街、ニューヨークの
ブロードウェイ地区に建設されたビル

Constructed in the Broadway district
of New York, the city Renzo Piano
described as a petrified forest of
constantly-changing light and reflection.

外観　Exterior

ビル入口　Building entrance

ザ・シャード　（2000-2012年）
The Shard - London Bridge Tower

8断面のガラスを組み合わせた72層建て
地上309.6mのタワー。240mの位置に、
スカイラインの遊歩道と展望台がある

Tower rising to 309.6m, with eight glass facades
and seventy-two stories.
Includes an open air sky deck and public
viewing gallery 240m above the ground.

《宇宙に捧ぐ》(2001年)　*Hommage au Cosmos* (2001)

《光の雲》(2004年)　*Cloud of Light* (2004)

地上で最高のものを創る
Best in the world

────── ジャン＝ルイ・デュマ　Jean-Louis Dumas

作品を作るのではなく空間を創る
Create a space instead of making a work

────── 新宮晋　Susumu Shingu

07 ｜ コラボレーション　Collaborations

銀座メゾンエルメス ＋ 宇宙に捧ぐ
Ginza Maison Hermès ＋ *Hommage au Cosmos*

■ 2001 ［64歳(age)］

銀座にあるフランスのファッションメゾン、エルメスの日本店舗兼オフィス、アトリエ、アート・ギャラリー。晴海通りに面しては10mの幅しかなく、小径（ソニー通り）側に56mの奥行のある地上12階、地下3階建ての建物。56m幅のファサードの方に、最上部から新宮晋の彫刻が、ちょうど二つの棟が連なり建物がセットバックした箇所に設置されている。

The Japanese branch and offices for the French maison of Hermès in Ginza incorporates ateliers and an art gallery. Only 10m wide on its Harumi Avenue frontage, the building runs back 56m along a quiet side street (Sony Street), rising eleven stories high above ground, with three levels below ground. Sculpture work by Susumu Shingu hangs down from the top of the building at the center of the 56m facade, where it is set back from the street as the two halves of the building meet.

デザイン・工期 (Design and Construction)：1998–2006

08 ｜ コラボレーション　Collaborations

イル・ソーレ24オーレ本社 ＋ 光の雲
"Il Sole 24 Ore" Headquarters ＋ Cloud of Light

■ 2004 ［67歳(age)］

1960年代に建造されたビルを修復し、イタリアを代表する日刊経済新聞「イル・ソーレ24オーレ」の新本部へと改装したもの。広い中庭は丘陵として構想された建築設計の中心となるスペースであり、中庭からアトリウムを通って大通りへと抜けることもできる。この吹き抜け空間に新宮晋の彫刻が天井から設置されている。

RPBW restored this building that was constructed in the 1960s, and converted it into the new headquarters of the leading Italian financial daily newspaper *Il Sole 24 Ore*. A vast central garden serves as a space forming the center of an architectural design conceived as a hill, with the central garden offering access to the main road via an atrium. Sculpture work by Susumu Shingu hangs from the ceiling of this atrium space.

デザイン・工期 (Design and Construction)：1998–2005

ソニー通り側入口
Entrance on Sony Street side

イル・ソーレ24オーレ本社
"Il Sole 24 Ore" Headquarters

オランダのダンスカンパニー、ネザーランド・ダンス・シアター
（NDT）の振付師イリ・キリアンの依頼により
「トス・オブ・ア・ダイス」の舞台装置を手掛ける

Handles stage design for "Toss of a Dice" at the request of
Jiří Kylián, artistic director and choreographer of
the Dutch dance company Nederlands Dans Theater（NDT）

トス・オブ・ア・ダイス（2005年） "Toss of a Dice" (2005)

パリの個展で、自然エネルギーだけで自活できる村「呼吸する大地」の
構想を発表。風車のプロトタイプが完成し、長期テストを開始

Announces a plan for a village, Breathing Earth, that can support itself on natural energy alone
at a solo exhibition in Paris. Completes a prototype for the windmills, and begins long-term testing.

[左]「呼吸する大地」ジオラマ（2009年）　[右]「呼吸する大地」風車（2009年）
Left : Breathing Earth, Diorama (2009)
Right : Breathing Earth, Windmill (2009)

6年間の密着取材の末、
『ブリージング・アース─新宮 晋の夢』
（監督トーマス・リーデルスハイマー）が完成。
ルーブル美術館、ナポリの
映画祭をはじめ全国で上映

The documentary film
Breathing Earth – Susumu Shingu's Dream
directed by Thomas Riedelsheimer is completed
after six years of close coverage.
It is shown at the Louvre, the Naples International
Film Festival, and throughout Japan.

新宮晋 風のミュージアム
Susumu Shingu WIND MUSEUM

三田市の県立有馬富士公園内に「新宮晋 風のミュージアム」が
オープン。12点の彫刻が野外で常設展示される

The Susumu Shingu Wind Museum opens in Arimafuji Park
in Sanda City, with twelve sculptures on permanent exhibit outdoors

2005~ ［68歳（age）~］

2006~ ［69歳（age）~］

中庭から見た甲羅状の屋根　Carapace-like roof seen from the courtyard

ジェローム・セドゥ・パテ財団 （2006-2014年）
Jérôme Seydoux Pathé Foundation

パリ13区に建てられたマルチ・シネマで有名な
ジェローム・セドゥ・パテ財団の新本部で
映画アーカイブを有する展示上映施設

New headquarters building built in
the XIII arrondissement of Paris
for the Jérôme Seydoux Pathé Foundation,
including the foundation's archives
and associated screening facility.

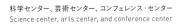

コロンビア大学
マンハッタンビル・キャンパス

（2002-2018年、アメリカ、ニューヨーク）
Manhattanville Campus of
Columbia University

科学センター、芸術センター、コンフェレンス・センター
Science center, arts center, and conference center

ホイットニー美術館 （2007-2015年、アメリカ、ニューヨーク）
The Whitney Museum of American Art

[左] ガンセボート通りからの夜景　[右] ガラスのファサードと屋外階段のある北側
Left : View from Gansevoort Street at night　Right : North side with glass façade and exterior staircases

エマージェンシー小児外科病院 （2013-2020年、ウガンダ、エンテベ）
EMERGENCY Children's Surgical Hospital, Entebbe, Uganda

建物全景写真
Entire building

特徴的な版築土の壁、屋根と柱
Distinctive rammed earth walls
and roofs and columns

アカデミー映画博物館 （2012-2020年）
Academy Museum of Motion Pictures

パリ裁判所 （2010-2017年、フランス、パリ）
Paris Courthouse

東に面したファサード
East-facing façade

アカデミー映画博物館　全体写真
Academy Museum of Motion Pictures overall view

ロサンゼルス中心部に建設されたアカデミー映画博物館。
球体のビルには、客席千席の劇場展望テラスがある。

Situated in the heart of Los Angeles.
A new spherical building includes a 1,000-seat
theater and a terrace with views of the city
and the HOLLYWOOD hills.

185

［上］《神話》 ［下左］《叙事詩》 ［下右］《宇宙》（2016年）
Top : Myth　Bottom left : Epic　Bottom right : Cosmos (2016)

時空を超えて
Beyond time and space

—— 新宮晋　Susumu Shingu

09 ｜ コラボレーション　Collaborations

スタヴロス・ニアルコス財団文化センター ＋ 宇宙、叙事詩、神話
Stavros Niarchos Foundation Cultural Center ＋ Cosmos, Epic, Myth

■ 2016 ［79歳（age）］

アテネから南に4kmの地点にあるカリテアに建設されたギリシャ国立図書館と国立オペラ劇場を有する巨大文化センター。図書館と劇場はパブリックスペース「アゴラ」によって繋がれた。図書館と劇場、パブリックスペースにそれぞれ新宮晋の彫刻が合計3作品、天井から吊ってある。2016年10月LEED最高賞であるプラチナ賞受賞。

This enormous cultural center comprising the National Library of Greece and the Greek National Opera was constructed in Kallithea, 4km south of central Athens. The opera house and library are connected by a public space, known as the Agora. One sculpture each by Susumu Shingu is suspended from the ceiling in the opera house, library, and public space. In October 2016, the complex obtained the highest level of LEED certification, platinum certification.

デザイン・工期（Design and Construction）：2008-2016

運河側から人口丘と建物を見る
Artificial hill and building viewed from the canal side

レンゾ・ピアノのスケッチ（2014年）
Renzo Piano sketch (2014)

186

フランスのシャンボール城で、
レオナルド・ダ・ヴィンチ没後500年を記念した個展
「新宮晋—現代のユートピア」展を開催

Holds the solo exhibition *Une utopie d'aujourd'hui* (*A Utopia for Today*) at the Château de Chambord in France in commemoration of the 500th anniversary of the death of Leonardo da Vinci.

「新宮 晋－現代のユートピア」
シャンボール城（2019年）
"Une utopie d'aujourd'hui
(A Utopia Today)" at the
Château de Chambord (2019)

オリジナルキャラクター「サンダリーノ」を考案。
同キャラクターによるポップアップ絵本を
世界3カ国（フランス、イタリア、日本）で出版

Conceives of the character Sandalino, and publishes pop-up books based on it in France, Italy, and Japan.

絵本『サンダリーノ　どこから来たの？』（2019年）
Picture book, *Sandalino, where came from?*

2019〜 ［82歳（age）〜］

2018〜 ［81歳（age）〜］

ジェノヴァ・サン・ジョルジョ橋（2018-2020年、イタリア、ジェノヴァ）
Genova San Giorgio Bridge

［左］全体写真　［右］橋を下から眺める
Left : Overall view　Right : Bridge viewed from underneath

ジェノヴァのポルチェーベラ川にかかる橋。ジェノヴァと全イタリアを繋ぐ交通の要であり、2018年に老朽化のため崩壊したモランディ橋に代わるものとして急ピッチで新設された

New bridge over the Polcevera in Genoa.
The city's role as a key hub for the whole of Italy required rapid construction to replace the aged Morandi bridge that collapsed in 2018.

「Renzo Piano The Art of Making Buildings」展を
ロンドンのロイヤル・アカデミー・オブ・アーツで開催
（2018-2019年、イギリス、ロンドン）

会場風景（2018年）　Installation view (2018)

Renzo Piano : The Art of Making Buildings exhibition at the Royal Academy of Arts in London

《虹色の葉》(2021年)　*Rainbow Leaves* (2021)

クモは天才建築家
Spiders are genius architects

——— 新宮晋　Susumu Shingu

10 ｜ コラボレーション　Collaborations

565ブルーム・ソーホー ＋ 虹色の葉
565 Broome SoHo ＋ Rainbow Leaves

■ **2021** [84歳(age)]

ニューヨークのソーホー地区に建てられた高層マンションで「565ブルーム」とは建物のある通りの名前から。30階建ての建物からは、ハドソン川とニューヨークの景観が見渡せる。細いマリオンとファサードの曲線ガラスが、ビルの内と外の境界線を曖昧にして内部を光で満ち溢れさせる。二つの棟の空隙に新宮晋の彫刻がある。

565 Broome SoHo is a high-rise condominium residence constructed at 565 Broome Street in New York's Soho neighborhood. The 30-story structure provides sweeping views of the Hudson River and New York. The slim mullions and the curved glass in the facade blur the boundaries between inside and outside, and fill the inside of the building with light. A sculpture by Susumu Shingu is installed in the opening between the two towers.

デザイン・工期 (Design and Construction)：2014-2019

565ブルーム・ソーホー＋《虹色の葉》
565 Broome SoHo + *Rainbow Leaves*

恵まれた自然環境の中で、
楽しみながら学び、創造する
「地球アトリエ」の
プロジェクトがスタート

Starts activities related to *Atelier Earth*,
a place for creating things while having fun
and playing in a wonderful natural environment.

地球アトリエ ATELIER EARTH

元気のぼり　*Genki Nobori*

新宮晋
Susumu Shingu

2023～ [86歳(age)～]

未来へ
To the future

2023～ [86歳(age)～]

完成予想図
Rendering of completed project

レンゾ・ピアノ
Renzo Piano

東京海上ビルディング
（2019-、日本、東京）
Tokio Marine Building,
2019-in progress, Tokyo, Japan

東京・丸の内に建造される東京海上グループの新社屋ビル。木とガラスの外観が特徴的で、木材の使用量はビルとしては最大規模となる。2028年竣工予定

The new headquarter building for
Tokio Marine Group in Marunouchi,
featuring wood/glass exterior and using wood on
an unprecedented scale. Due for completion in 2028.

地球アトリエ
Atelier Earth

「新宮晋 風のミュージアム」を主な活動ステージとして、世界中からアーティストや文学者、科学者や生物学者たちが集い、国籍、性別、世代に関係なく市民一人ひとりと一緒に地球の未来の生き方を考え、発表しようという活動が、今まさに進行形で行われている。最初の構想発表は2019年秋、フランス・シャンボール城で「新宮 晋 — 現代のユートピア」展として開催された。「ウインドサーカス」から「ウインドキャラバン」、そして「呼吸する大地（ブリージング・アース）」へと着実に歩みを進め、辿り着いた先に浮かんだキーワードが「ユートピア」だった。一人ひとりが地球をみんなのアトリエだと考えれば争いはなくなるはずだ。新宮にとってのユートピア、それが「地球アトリエ」なのだ。「風のアーティスト」新宮晋の世界観を具現化するプロジェクトである。

Atelier Earth uses the Susumu Shingu Wind Museum as the primary stage for its activities. The aim is to create a place where artists, literary figures, scientists, and biologists can gather together with individual citizens, irrespective of nationality, gender, and age, to think about how we should live on the earth in the future, and to publish or present the thinking that results. Activities like these are now actively in progress. The first event was *Susumu Shingu : A Utopia for Today*, an exhibition held at Chambord, France in autumn 2019. Following the steady progression from *Windcircus* to *Wind Caravan* and *Breathing Earth*, the first keyword that came to Shingu's mind was "utopia." He realized that if we each think of the world as everyone's studio, we ought to be able to stop fighting. To Shingu, utopia was *Atelier Earth*. It is his project for giving shape to the worldview of Susumu Shingu, sculptor of the wind.

「地球アトリエ」は、大自然の中の複合文化施設として構想された。劇場、アートセンター、アトリエ、カフェやレストラン、ショップなどから成る。ここでは、様々な分野で活躍するアーティストや科学者、文学者等と地球の未来のあり方を考え、話し合い、発信する。同時に、ものを作り芸術を創造する実践・実験の場でもある。緑と湖、星空の美しい自然の中で、垣根を設けず誰でも参加でき、アートの力が人の心と心を結びつける理想的な空間である。

Atelier Earth was conceived as a cultural complex situated in a rich natural environment. It includes a theater, art center, studio, café-restaurant, and shop. It is a place for thinking about how we should live in the future – in conjunction with people active in a variety of areas, including artists, scientists, and literary figures – for discussing such thoughts, and for conveying them to a broader audience. At the same time, it is a place for practicing and experimenting with making things and creating art. Surrounded by the beauty of nature, including greenery, the lake, and starry skies, it is an idealistic space without barriers, allowing anyone to join in, and employing the power of art to link hearts and minds together.

地球アトリエ ATELIER EARTH

PROJECT DATA

所在地	日本、兵庫
制作年	2019年 – 進行中

Location	Hyogo, Japan
Production	2019 – in progress

「地球アトリエ」シャンボール城（2019年）　*Atelier Earth*, at the Château de Chambord (2019)

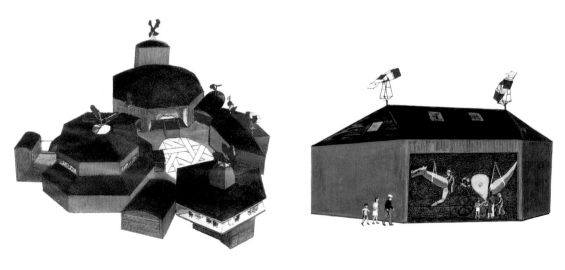

［左］「地球アトリエ」全体図　［右］アトリエスケッチ　*Left : Atelier Earth*, plan　*Right : Atelier Earth*, atelier sketch

サンダリーノとは？　Who is Sandalino?

サンダリーノは、雷といっしょに地球にやってきた、地球が大好きな宇宙人。
仲良くなった子どもたちといっしょに大活躍をする。絵本にコンサートに、子ども狂言。

Sandalino is an alien who comes to Earth with a stroke of lightning. He is fascinated by the various lives on Earth and quickly becomes friends with all the children. Sandalino makes his appearance in picture books, concerts and *kyogen* with children.

「地球アトリエ」サンダリーノの里 (2023年)　*Atelier Earth*, plan (2023)

元気のぼり　*Genki-nobori*

「元気のぼり」は、子どもたちが元気いっぱいの絵を、鯉のぼりの形の白い布に描くプロジェクト。
掲揚されて風をはらむと、それを見る人たちに元気のメッセージが伝わる。
新宮は「元気のぼり」こそ究極の風のアートと考えている。風には国境も人種差別の壁もない。
新宮は、世界中の子どもたちがいっしょになって「元気のぼり」の輪を広げるプロジェクトを計画している。

Genki-nobori is a project in which children draw colorful pictures on large pieces of white cloth in the shape of carp streamers.
When they are hoisted and fill with wind, they convey greetings and messages of love to everyone who sees them.
Shingu believes that *genki-nobori* is the ultimate wind art. The wind knows no borders or cultural barriers.
Shingu is planning a project in which children from all over the world will work together to expand the circle of *genki-nobori*.

東京海上ビルディング
Tokio Marine Building

2028年に竣工予定の東京海上グループの新しい本店ビル。2021年、RPBWが株式会社三菱地所設計と共に本プロジェクトのデザインを担当することが発表された。2022年10月、旧ビルの解体が開始、新ビルの着工は2024年12月に予定されている。建物の高さは旧ビルと同じ約100mで、地下3階、地上20階、塔屋2階のビルとなる予定。既存の高層ビルには見られないほど木材をふんだんに使用したビルで、ガラスと木材による7本の柱のファサードが特徴である。大木が豊かな葉をつけたかのように屋上には緑溢れる庭園が計画され、立方体の建築平面の中央の「パティオ（中庭）」、建物の周辺にも樹木が植えられる。東京駅近くの「丸の内」地区の都会の中心に、まるで森林のようなビルが誕生する。

The new headquarter building for Tokio Marine Group is scheduled for completion in 2028. In 2021, RPBW announced that it would be responsible for the design of this project in collaboration with Mitsubishi Jisho Design, Inc. Demolition of the old building began in October 2022, and work on constructing its replacement is scheduled to start in December 2024. Like the old building, the new headquarters will be around 100m tall, and it will have three basement floors, twenty floors above ground, and a two-story penthouse. It will make great use of timber, to an extent unprecedented in existing high-rise buildings, and will have a distinctive glass facade with seven wooden pillars. A lush green garden is also planned on the roof, as if great trees have burst into leaf, and trees will be planted in a patio within the architectural cube as well as around the exterior. This will create a building resembling a verdant woodland in the middle of the Marunouchi district close to Tokyo Station.

木材には最新技術で耐火性が付与された国産木材を用い、柱のみならず床材にもCLT（直行集成板）が使用される。建築を特徴づけるガラスのファサードは、歴史あるこの街の日々の営みを季節の移り変わり毎に映し出し、東京駅から皇居を繋ぐ新たな街並みのひとつとなる。レンゾ・ピアノとクライアントが繊細に議論を重ねて生み出されたコンセプトである。

Wood produced in Japan made fire-resistant using the latest technology is being used in the building, with cross laminated timber (CLT) used in both the columns and the flooring. The glass façade is a characteristic feature of the design, and will reflect the daily activity of this historic area from season to season, becoming a new part of the cityscape connecting Tokyo Station and the Imperial Palace. The concept was conceived through repeated, in-depth discussion between Renzo Piano and the client.

完成予想図 南西から
Rendering of completed project, viewed from south west

PROJECT DATA

所在地	日本、東京
工 期	2019年 – 進行中

Location	Tokyo, Japan
Construction	2019 – in progress

完成予想図　西側ファサード　Rendering of completed project, west façade

［上］屋上庭園の完成予想図　［下］地上階のピアッツァ（広場）の完成予想図　*Top* : Rendering of the roof garden　*Bottom* : Rendering of Piazza at ground floor

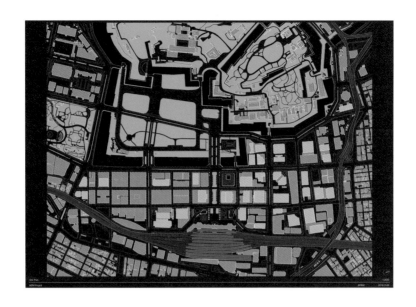

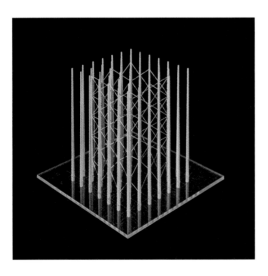

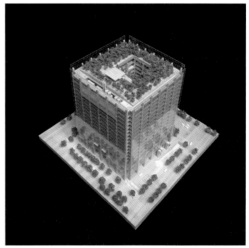

［上］完成予定地　赤色の場所がビル竣工予定地
［中］模型　完成予定地とビル
［下左］模型　コンセプト
［下右］模型　最終プラン

Top : Site and surroundings. Site of new building is marked in red.
Middle : Model of site with new building
Bottom left : Model of concept
Bottom right : Model of final plan

スタジオ・アッズーロ　Studio Azzurro

私たちスタジオ・アッズーロは、1982年以降、ビデオアート、劇場、映画、ヴィジュアル・ナレーションなどにおいて、あらゆる形態の技術的表現を実験してきた。スタジオ・アッズーロはソフトウェアとハードウェアを創造することによりルネサンス時代の「ボッテーガ（職人工房）」の伝統を実行し、テクノロジーを感じさせないようにしつつ鑑賞者との間にインタラクティヴな関係性を創り出すべく、全ての仕事を計画している。常にスタジオ・アッズーロはギャラリーやコレクターによる従来のアートマーケットを拒絶したデジタル・アート・エンヴァイロメントを生み出し、「美術館」における芸術体験という主流の枠組みを再定義し続ける。要するに、私たちの仕事は、その成果や観者との関係性のみならず、アーティスト、技術、芸術作品の関係性に対して問題提起するべく計画されているということである。

スタジオ・アッズーロの詩心は、こうした唯一無二の芸術的プロセスの創造へ寄与してきた多くの肉体と精神に宿る。多くのアーティストがパーソナリティと技量が相互に絡み合う新たな技術的言語の複雑性に直面している。スタジオ・アッズーロはそれ故に、他のアーティストやあらゆるグループとのコラボレーションに対して開かれている。

Since 1982 we have experimented with all forms of technological expression in video art, theater, film as well as visual narration. By creating our own software and hardware we operate in the tradition of a Renaissance "bottega" (artisan laboratory), we design all of our works to both conceal the technology from the observer and create an interactive relationship with the viewer; all the while we produce digital art environments that reject the traditional market distribution through galleries and collectors, and also re-frame the mainstream "museum" experience of art. Our work, in a word, is designed to problematize the relationship between artists, technology and works of art as well as their fruition and relationship to the observer.

The poetic soul of Studio Azzurro lives in the many bodies and minds of those who have contributed to the creation of this unique artistic process. The plural artist confronts the complexity of new technological languages intertwining personalities with competencies. We are therefore open to collaborations with other artists and group work of any kind.

スタジオ・アッズーロ

ヴィデオ・エンヴァイロメント
（ヴィデオ・インスタレーション）

大阪中之島美術館 **2023**

Studio Azzurro

Video Environment
Nakanoshima Museum of Art, Osaka 2023

ジェノヴァ港再開発
Re-development of the Genoa Old Harbour

並んで進む様子を観察すると　　スタジオ・アッズーロ

突然の風にあおられたように、レンゾ・ピアノによるプロジェクトの模型が、プロジェクトシートやレイアウト、写真を解き放っていく。紙は空中で漂い、飛び去り、そして数枚は美術館の壁面にある大きな黒板の上に広げられると、物語を組み立て始める。上方に吊るされた新宮の作品は、その突風をあおり、空間と戯れるかのようだ。映像との絶え間ない対話が続く。

「平行人生」展の準備にあたってスタジオ・アッズーロは、想像力の二つの素晴しい過程の展開を驚きながら並べて、好奇心あふれる観察者として取り組んだ。どちらの場合も、イマジネーションは風を入れ替えるが、常に「何かと」、とりわけ自然の中にある何かと関係している。注意深い観察によって、また不可視の法則に関する深い知識によって育まれたイマジネーション。レンゾ・ピアノと新宮晋のプロジェクトにおける並外れた軽さは、研究され、吸収され、翼のある詩的思考に奉仕する諸法則を垣間見えるままにさせ、諸法則を乗り越え、そしてむしろ諸法則を応用するかのようである。諸法則適用のための調査研究は少なく、地球の生命体や鉱物の形態の中にその存在は表明されている。言葉を用いずに、レンゾ・ピアノと新宮晋は世界の目に見えない仕組みを語るのだ。

新宮とピアノのスケッチや写真、図面などのシートからは二人の作品の表面上の簡潔性の裏に隠されたその偉大な研究と電光のような統合が透けてみえる。デッサンやスケッチは「場所」であり、そこで諸法則は洗練された強さをもって、自らの正体を明かす。シートは、思考を集め可視世界と接触させ、非物質を集め物質と接触させる表面なのである。シートを裏返すだけで、思考は再び見えなくなり、近寄れなくなる。

スタジオ・アッズーロにとって、ヴィデオは常に、空間と基本的な関係をもつための装置であり、それは空間を変えることができ、光や音が物理的なものと投影される映像の画面の境界線を解体し溶かしながらイメージが現れるあの暗闇の存在の複合性によって、複数の次元を形作るに十分なものであった。ここで私たちは、二人の平行人生のために、新宮の作品の「帆」を動かしレンゾ・ピアノの建築における透明性をくすぐるのと同じ風を鑑賞者に感じさせる環境で、二人の作品の物としての存在感を強調することを意図した。

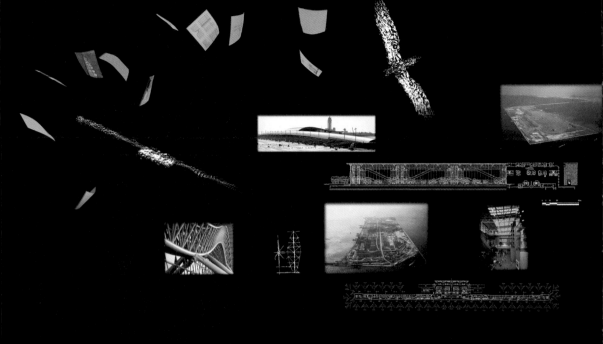

Observing in parallel   Studio Azzurro

As if fanned by a sudden gust of wind, the scale models of projects by Renzo Piano spill out project documents, layouts, and photographs. These sheets of paper float around and fly away, with some of them opening out on a large blackboard installed on the museum wall, where they begin to compose a story. Works by Susumu Shingu suspended above appear to be stirred by the wind and cavort in the space in a continual dialog with moving images.

Studio Azzurro approached the preparations for Parallel Lives as a curious observer, watching with amazement when extending two awesome paths of the imagination side by side. In both cases, the imagination involves the air and the winds passing through, but always remains in touch with "things"— and particularly with nature. The imagination is nurtured by careful observation and a deep knowledge of invisible laws. The unusual lightness conveyed by the projects of Renzo Piano and Susumu Shingu provides glimpses of such laws, which have been learned, absorbed, and put to the service of poetical thoughts with wings, enabling the laws to be transcended and, conversely, applied.

This less studied way of adopting those laws clearly reveals their presence in the lifeforms and minerals of our planet. Wordlessly, Renzo Piano and Susumu Shingu tell us of the unseen fabric that holds our world together.

However, the extensive studies and sharp analysis that can be glimpsed from the airborne project documents are concealed behind the superficial simplicity of Piano and Shingu' s works. Detailed sketches and drawings are places where the sophisticated strength of their lows bears witness to the reality. A piece of paper is a surface that attracts thoughts and links them to the visible world; bringing the immaterial into contact with material. Simply turning the paper over would take the thoughts out of sight again, making them inaccessible.

To Studio Azzurro, video is always a mechanism for entering into a fundamental relationship with a space in order to transform the space and mold its dimensions with the help of light, sound, and the presence of physical objects and darkness from which images can emerge, dispelling the rigid frame of screenings. What we desired for these two parallel lives was to be able to emphasize the physical presence of Shingu and Piano' s work in an environment where visitors feel they are carried by the same wind that moves the "sails" of Shingu' s works and touches the transparency of Piano's architecture.

レンゾ・ピアノ・ビルディング・ワークショップ（ジェノヴァ）
Renzo Piano Building Workshop（Genoa）

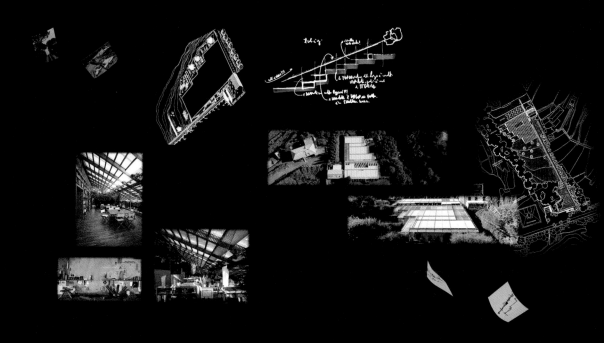

銀座メゾンエルメス
Ginza Maison Hermès

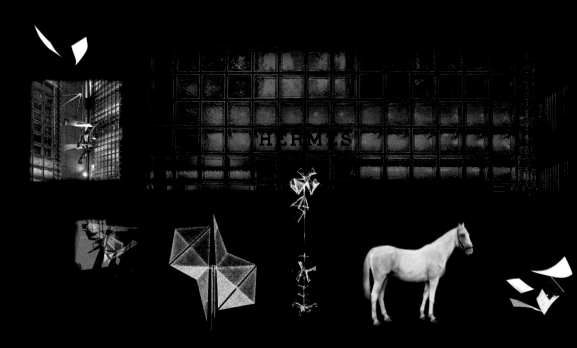

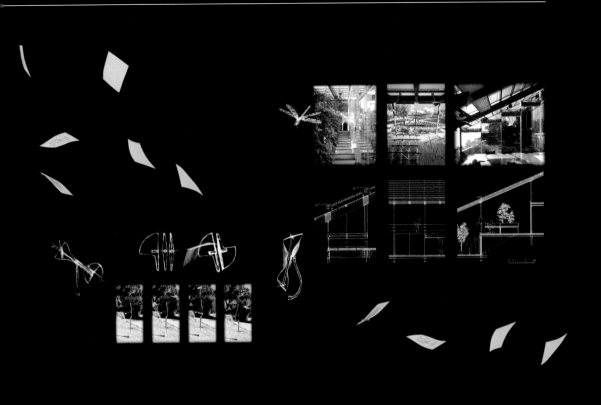

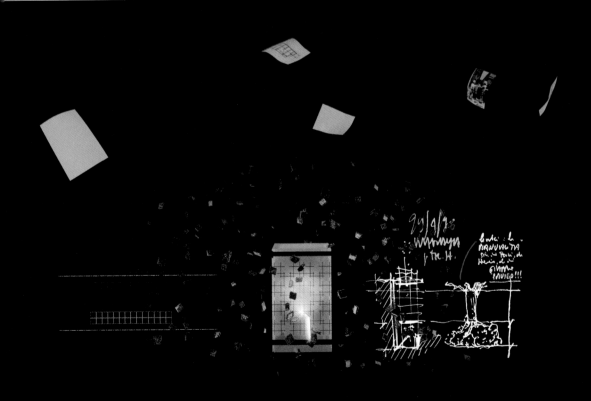

565ブルーム・ソーホー

565 Broome SoHo

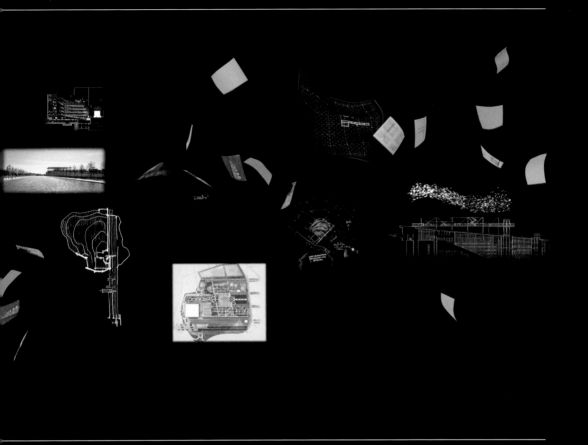

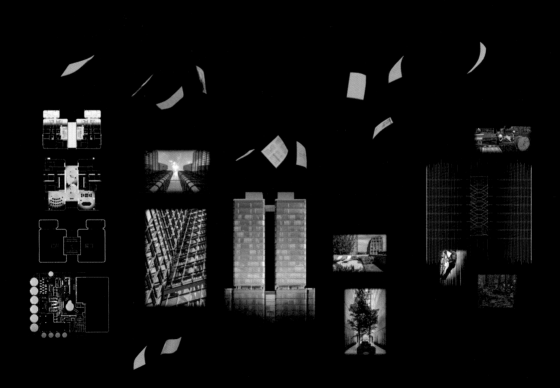

ポンピドー・センター
Centre Georges Pompidou

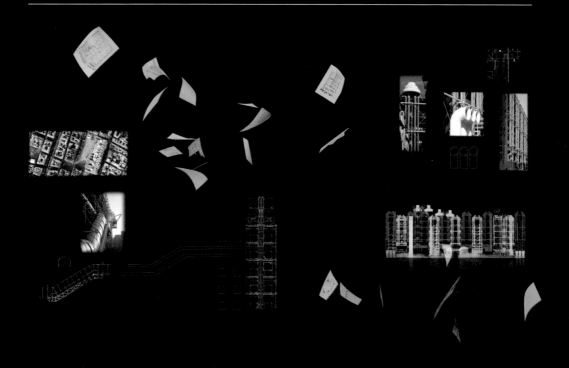

IBMトラベリング・パビリオン
IBM Traveling Pavilion

チバウ文化センター
Jean-Marie Tjibaou Cultural Center

ザ・シャード
The Shard - London Bridge Tower

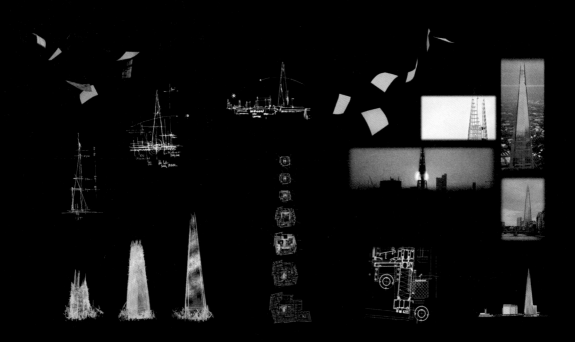

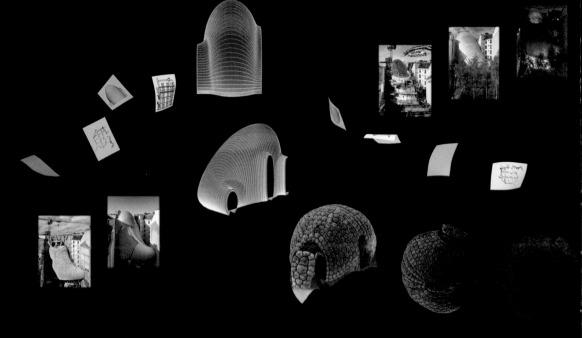

アカデミー映画博物館
Academy Museum of Motion Pictures

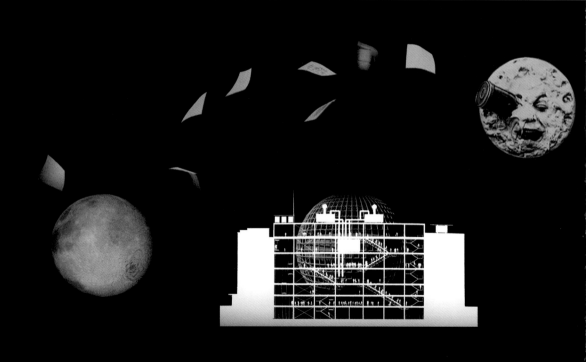

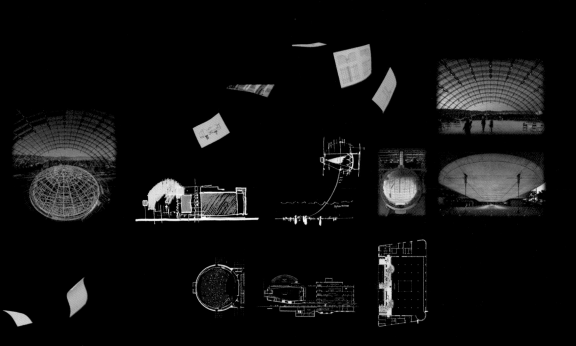

平行人生

私の名前はレンゾ・ピアノ、私は建築家だ。新宮晋とはずいぶん長い付き合いになる。私たちは非常に親しい友人で、同じ年だ。表面上はかけ離れた人生を送っていても、思いがけない近さというものは存在する。それはまさしく私と晋に起こったことだ。というのは、私たちは80年代末に大阪で初めて会ったが、お互いに長年の知り合いであるかのような印象をもった。ずっと昔から知っているようだった。それぞれが異なる観点からの展望を抱いていても、同じ願いを求め、同じ夢を追うときにそうしたことが起こる。それはまた、心配事や熱望、好奇心に関して似通ったものをもつときだ。運命を導くという赤い糸、そしてこの細い謎めいた糸は、人間関係において、各人の職業や出自、人生での経験を超え、人と人とを結びつけるものとして存在している。お互いにひきつけられるのは、対極にいるからではなく、似ているからなのだ。

オクタビオ・パス※1は詩について話すことで、このことをうまく述べていた。すなわち、偶然の所産なのだが、計算の結実であると。これはあらゆる人間の活動に、そして似通った魂に関わるなら、あらゆる出会いに当てはまる。私たちが一緒に仕事をするたびに、新宮晋は小さな魔法を実現した。プロジェクトは合理的なものと非合理的なもの、実用主義と理想主義、それから具体性と空想を混ぜ合わせたものだ。建築物を設計することは、最初から最後まで現実に即したひとつの道だが、予期しない、驚くべきなにかを欲する瞬間がある。こうしたときに、新宮との調律が合って、まさに私が探していたなにかに答えが与えられる。私がすべきなのは、待つことに尽きる。風は目に見えないが、新宮は彼の作品によって、それを目に見えるものにする。水は移ろいやすく、形がないが、新宮はそれに形を与える。彼は芸術家であり、職人であり、辛抱強く控えめな技術者であり、そして動きの魔術師なのだ。私たちはどちらも、重力に対して絶え間なく挑戦して、軽さを用いて仕事をする。こうした作品としては、関西国際空港の天井に吊るされた巨大な帆やジェノヴァのポルト・アンティーコ、東京にあるエルメスの店舗※2やアテネのスタヴロス・ニアルコス財団文化センターにあるオペラハウス、そして最近では、ニューヨークのソーホー地区にある高層ビルといったところに置かれた彫刻が挙げられる。新宮の仕事は私の日々においても、変わらず存在していて、私がジェノヴァやパリにいても、仕事場や自宅にいても、いつもそこに私たちに通じるものを証明する彫刻がある。

バランス感覚は、人間には生まれたときから、子どもの頃の一番最初の記憶から備わっているものだ。晋の仕事に立ち会うことはこれらの最初の時点、つまり私の根源に私を戻す。というのは、子どもの頃にはそんなことは考えないものだが、私たちくらいの年になると自分たちがすでにしたことではなく、まだやるべきことこそが自らを生き生きとした状態に保たせる。若者になるにはたくさんの時間が必要なのだ。

建築家　レンゾ・ピアノ

※注1　1914-1998年、メキシコの詩人、批評家、外交官　　※注2　銀座メゾンエルメス

Parallel Lives

My name is Renzo Piano, and I am an architect. I have known Susumu Shingu for ages. We are close friends, and we are the same age. People may apparently live very different lives, but be close in unexpected ways. That's how it is with me and Susumu. When we first met at the end of the 1980s in Osaka, we both had the impression that we had known each other for a long time; that we had always known each other. That happens when two people have the same desires and are pursuing the same dreams, even though they have different perspectives. It happens when they have similar anxieties, similar aspirations, and similar curiosity. People can be linked by a thin red line, a thread that is both subtle and mysterious, joining people beyond their professions, their roots, and the experiences in their lives. It is not their differences that draw them together, but their similarities.

Octavio Paz (1914-1998, Mexican poet, critic, and diplomat) described poetry as the "result of chance; fruit of calculation." That is very insightful, and the same thing can be said of every human activity and encounter when two minds strongly resemble each other. Every time we worked together on something, Susumu Shingu produced a little magic. Projects are a mix of the rational and the irrational, of pragmatism and idealism, and of concreteness and dreams. The design process for architecture remains solidly realistic from start to finish, but there are moments when you feel the need for something unexpected, something surprising. That is when the harmony with Shingu comes into play, and he is always able to come up with a response that fits what I am looking for. All I have to do is wait. The wind is invisible, but Shingu can produce works that make it visible. Water is transient and without form, but Shingu can give it form. He is an artist, an artisan, a patient and unpretentious technician, and a magician of movement. We both work with lightness, constantly challenging the force of gravity. Look at for example the enormous sails suspended from the ceiling of Kansai International Airport, and his sculptures for Genoa's Porto Antico, the Maison Hermès flagship store in Ginza, Tokyo, the Opera House in the Stavros Niarchos Cultural Center in Athens, and, more recently, at the residential towers in Soho, New York. Yet, his works are also a constant presence in my daily life. Whether I am in Genoa or Paris, at home or at work, there is always one of Shingu's sculptures bearing witness to the convergence of our paths.

Humans are born with a sense of balance, and it is a part of our earliest memories. Attending to Susumu's work takes me back to those earliest moments, returning me to my roots. We did not think about it when we were kids, but when you get to our age, what keeps us alive is not what you have done with your life, but what you still have to do. It takes a long time to become young !

Architect, Renzo Piano

風の設計 ── 新宮 晋 ＋ レンゾ・ピアノ

姿見えざるは之即ち風である乎？　然り、之即ち風である。何となれば姿が見えないではない乎。
これ風以外の何物でもあり得ない。風である。然り風である風である風である。[※1]（坂口安吾「風博士」より）

早20年以上前のことになるが、私がミラノに留学していた頃、建築史の学生たちの間で話題になっていたのが、
レンゾ・ピアノの建築がミラノの近くローディという町にあるよ、今度は銀行の建物を作ったよ、というものだった。
ローディ……？　聞きなれない町の名前だったが、ともかく行ってみることにした。たしかミラノから鉄道でそう
遠くない、各駅停車の便しか止まらない町だったと思う。鉄道駅を降りるとすぐ近くに新しい美術館があって
ちょうどル・コルビュジエの絵画展をやっていた。そのすぐ近くに、バンカ・ポポラーレ・ディ・ローディはあった。
銀行の建物のため、一般の訪問者でも自由に周囲を歩いて見て回ることができた。いや、今となっては銀行
の建物だからではなく、レンゾ・ピアノが外に開かれた建築として構想したからだったと分かったが。建物の
外を歩いて回って、ふと中庭に入ったとき、空気がサアっと変わったような気がした。この建築を特徴づける
円形の透明の庇から光がふりそそぎ、風が流れる。外から眺めた印象とは異なる別の中庭が広がっていた。
この中庭に新宮晋の《水の花》がある。

この感覚が何なのかすぐには飲み込めなかったが、この後、フィレンツェでブルネレスキが設計したパッツィ
礼拝堂に入ったとき同じ感覚を抱いた。実際の建物としての物質性とその建物の中で人が受ける感覚
の違いは、一体何なのか。レンゾ・ピアノの建築には、目に見えない何かがある、そう思った。イタリア語で
「アリオーゾ」という言葉を知ったのを知ったのはこの後からだったと思う。「空気（アーリア）」から派生
した形容詞で、「風通しのよい、広々とした、のびやかな」の意味がある。

「空気の流れを見えるようにしてくれないか」──これが、レンゾ・ピアノが関西国際空港の仕事で新宮晋
に最初にコラボレーションを持ち掛けたときの言葉だったという。

関西国際空港は日本初の本格的な国際コンペとしても歴史上重要性が高く、参加希望者は48者、内15者
が設計競技参加者として指名された。1988年12月9日RPBWパリの案が最優秀作品に選出され、1989年
3月24日RPBWジャパン、パリ空港公団、日建設計、日本空港コンサルタンツの4社で構成される関西国際
空港旅客ターミナルビル基本設計作成共同企業体に基本設計が委託された。この企業体にオーヴ・アラップ
＆パートナーズ・インターナショナルがRPBWジャパンの協力事務所として加わり、日建設計と共に構造と設備
を担当する。1990年3月27日基本設計を実施した共同企業体と契約が結ばれ実施設計に着手、1991年3月
15日実施設計が完了している。若齢埋立地盤上に38カ月という短い工事期間で臨まれた、イタリア、フランス、
イギリス、日本の4カ国による日本初の本格的国際共同設計だった。

この建築を特徴づける天井のデザインの構想は基本設計時のさまざまなコンピューター・シミュレーション及び
イギリスのパークシャーでの10分の1模型を使った巨大空間におけるシミュレーションの成果であり、前例や
模範があったものではない。片側からエアを噴射することで空間全体の空気層が安定することも、このシミュ

レーションの中で分かったことだ。空気の流れの実験成果は、建築デザインにその都度反映されて、最終的に現状の形に仕上がっていったのである。こうした一連の広範な研究に携わった中心人物が構造家のピーター・ライス[2]と設備エンジニアのトム・ベーカーをチーフとするオーヴ・アラップ社のチームだった。

その後1993年2月、天井の構造体のモックアップ・テストが北海道製作工場で実施される。工事ではアルミフレームを工場で仮組した後、現場での組み立てと膜の取り付けが太陽工業によって行われた。テフロン膜は0.8mmと非常に薄いもので、アメリカのデュポン社製。このオープンエアダクト19本に水色のジェットノズルから毎秒7mの風が送り出されている。チェックインカウンター上部などに設置されたアッパーライトの光は、このテフロンコーティングのガラスクロスの膜に反射され、間接照明の役割も果たしている。この膜の下に、先のレンゾ・ピアノの言葉をきっかけとして、新宮晋は「グラム彫刻」を計画した。グラム彫刻とは新宮晋自身の命名で、一グラム単位にまでこだわって設計することによって小さな振動にも反応する動きを生み出そう、独自に考案されたものである。わずかな微風にも反応して動く彫刻のことだ。このグラム彫刻17体が、国際線出発フロアに吊り下げられている。二種類の長さがあり、長い方が14.3m、もう一方は12.77m。いずれも黄色と青色の帆のある彫刻が、レンゾ・ピアノによる建築の見えない特徴を語りつつ、今日もゆったりとした幸福な動きを続ける。

実際、風というのは目に見えない。かつて赤瀬川原平（1937-2014）は、扇風機を茶紙と紐で梱包し、《風》（1963年／再制作1985年、東京都現代美術館蔵）というタイトルをつけて造形芸術にしてみせた。人工的に風を起こす扇風機を包んで表現したように、目に見えない「風」というテーマは造形芸術になりにくい。しかしながら、本展の二人は、建築、そして彫刻というジャンルで、この目に見えない「風」を設計し、視覚化するというその無謀とも思える企てを行ってきた。まさしく夢と冒険。風のみならず、水、太陽、雲、植物など、二人は自然の諸物を常に念頭においており、人知を超えて自然とつながっている。二人の創造物のある世界はとても優しい。

大阪中之島美術館主任学芸員　平井 直子

※注1　坂口安吾「風博士」1931年、『坂口安吾全集　1』筑摩書房、1989年、46頁
※注2　ピーター・ライス：構造エンジニア。ポンピドー・センターの設計でオーヴ・アラップ社のチーフ・デザイン・エンジニアを務める。1976-80年、レンゾ・ピアノと石田俊二、岡部憲明とともにPIANO RICE ASSOCIATESを設立。1981年、R.F.R.事務所を設立。1992年に逝去するまでレンゾ・ピアノと協働した。

主要参考文献
『CONSTRUCTION of the KANSAI INTERNATIONAL AIRPORT PASSENGER TERMINAL BUILDING』関西国際空港株式会社 建設事務所建築課、1995年
『関西国際空港旅客ターミナルビル　レンゾ・ピアノ・ビルディング・ワークショップ』講談社、1994年

Designing the Wind : Susumu Shingu + Renzo Piano

Does being invisible mean it's the wind ? Yes, it has to be the wind.
It's invisible, so it can't be anything else but the wind. It's the wind. It has to be the wind, the wind, the wind.
*1 — Ango Sakaguchi, *Kaze Hakase* (Dr Wind)

More than twenty years ago, when I was studying in Milan, some of the history of architecture students were getting excited that Renzo Piano had designed a building nearby in Lodi. This time, they were saying, he had built a bank. Lodi … ? I'd never heard of the place before, but I decided to go and take a look. It certainly wasn't that far from Milan by train, and I think that only the local trains stopped there. When I came out of the station, right there was a new museum building showing an exhibition of Le Corbusier's pictures. And almost next door was the Banca Popolare de Lodi.

Because it was a bank, even general visitors could walk around it and take a look. No, I realize now that it wasn't because the building was a bank, but because Renzo Piano had conceptualized it as a structure open to the outside. After having wandered around the building's exterior, when I walked straight into the piazza, it seemed to me as if the air had suddenly changed. Light was pouring in through the circular, transparent canopy that is a feature of the building, and a breeze was blowing. The piazza that opened out before me gave quite a different impression from that obtained by looking from outside. And in the piazza is Susumu Shingu's *Water Flower*.

The feeling wasn't something that I could immediately understand, but when I later went into the Pazzi Chapel in Florence, designed by Brunelleschi, I got the same sensation. It made me wonder about the difference between the physicality of a building and the feeling the building gives people on entering it. I decided that Renzo Piano's architecture has something that cannot be seen by the naked eye. I think it was some time later that I learned the Italian word *arioso*. An adjective derived from the noun *aria* (air), its nuances include "airy, expansive, relaxed."

"Can you create something that will make the streams of air visible ?" That was how Renzo Piano approached Susumu Shingu with an invitation to collaborate in working on the Kansai International Airport.

Kansai International Airport is historically important in that it was Japan's first full-scale international architectural competition. Out of forty-eight aspiring entrants, fifteen were chosen to take part in the design competition. On December 9, 1988, the RPBW Paris proposal was selected as the final winner, and on March 24, 1989 the basic design was contracted to the Kansai International Airport Passenger Terminal Building Basic Design Preparation Consortium, consisting of the four companies of RPBW Japan, Aéroports de Paris, Nikken Sekkei, and Japan Airport Consultants, Inc. Ove Arup & Partners International was added to this consortium as a consultant to RPBW Japan, with joint responsibility for the structure and services together with Nikken Sekkei. On March 27, 1990, a contract was signed with the consortium responsible for the basic design and work was started on the final design, which was completed on March 15, 1991. This was Japan's first ever real international joint design project. It involved the four nations of Italy, France, the UK, and Japan, and the building work, on a newly constructed artificial island, was completed within the short time of thirty-eight months.

The form of the ceiling that is the defining characteristic of this architecture was developed at the preliminary design stage through a series of computer simulations and simulation tests of a 1:10 scale model in a massive space in Berkshire, UK. Such tests were essential because the concept was unprecedented. In particular, the simulations demonstrated that air projected from one side could ensure stable stratification of the air throughout the entire space. As the findings from the air flow tests emerged, they were applied to the architectural design, eventually resulting in the shape that can be seen today. These extensive studies were conducted by a team from Ove Arup, led by structural engineer Peter Rice[2] and services engineer Tom Barker.

Subsequently, in February 1993, mock-up tests of the structure of the ceiling were carried out at the Hokkaido fabrication plant. Following a trial assembly of the actual aluminum frame in the factory, it was assembled on-site and the membrane was fitted by Taiyo Kogyo. This Teflon membrane, made by DuPont in the United States, is only 0.8mm thick. Sky-blue jet nozzles blow air into the ceiling's nineteen open-air ducts at 7m per second. The illumination from the upper lights sited above the check-in desks and elsewhere is reflected from the Teflon-coated glass cloth membrane so that it also provides indirect illumination.

Below this membrane, inspired by the words of Renzo Piano quoted earlier, are Susumu Shingu's *gram sculptures*. The name was coined by Shingu himself, and refers to the fact that they are uniquely devised to a precision of a single gram, so that they move in response to even tiny fluctuations as a result of their finely tuned design. They also move with the faintest breaths of air. Seventeen of these *gram sculptures* hang in the international departures floor. They come in two different lengths, with the longer measuring 14.3m and the shorter 12.77m. Both are sculptures with yellow and blue sails. Providing dynamic testimony of the invisible characteristics of Renzo Piano's architecture, they still continue their leisurely, joyful movements today.

It's true that wind is invisible to our eyes. Genpei Akasegawa (1937-2014) once wrapped an electric fan in brown paper and string, and exhibited it as visual art under the title "Wind" (1963, recreated 1985, in the collection of the Museum of Modern Art, Tokyo). The invisible "wind" is a challenging subject for visual artists, as evidenced by the wrapping of an electric fan that creates an artificial breeze. However, the two individuals in this exhibition have both engaged in the seemingly foolhardy endeavor of designing and making visible this invisible wind in the genres of architecture and sculpture. It is truly a dream and an adventure. Renzo Piano and Susumu Shingu always bear in mind not just the wind, but other aspects of nature including water, sun, clouds, and plants, and are connected to the natural world in a manner that lies beyond human understanding. Their creations inhabit a deeply tender, gentle world.

Senior Curator, Nakanoshima Museum of Art, Osaka   Naoko Hirai

Notes
1. Ango Sakaguchi, *Kaze Hakase* (Dr Wind), 1931, "Collected Works of Sakaguchi Ango 1," Chikuma Shobo, 1989, p.46.
2. Peter Rice: Structural engineer who served as Ove Arup & Partners' chief design engineer for the Pompidou Center project. From 1976 to 1980, he worked with Renzo Piano, Shunji Ishida, and Noriaki Okabe as Piano Rice Associates, and in 1981, founded RFR. He worked with Renzo Piano right up to his death in 1992.

Main References
Construction of the Kansai International Airport Passenger Terminal Building. Department of Architecture, Construction Office, Kansai International Airport Corporation, 1995
Kansai International Airport Passenger Terminal: Renzo Piano Building Workshop. Kodansha, 1994

レンゾ・ピアノ《平行人生展のためのスケッチ》　Renzo Piano's *Sketch for Parallel Lives*

二つの平行人生のためのスケッチについての覚え書き
Notes on the drawing for two parallel lives

展示のための最初の打ち合わせの間に、レンゾ・ピアノがたちどころに描いたスケッチのひとつは、簡潔で啓発的なものだった。真っ直ぐでない不確かな線で、共に進行する二本がはっきりと示された縦向きの一枚のスケッチ。この二本の線は二つの行程であり、どんな電車も通りえない二本のレールである。なぜならどんな人生も真っ直ぐな線とはならず、どんな平行する人生も対をなすもう一方の人生から常に等距離であることはあり得ないからだ。新宮の線はピアノのより少し高い位置の、オレンジ色で塗りつぶされたハート形に似た丸から始まって、そのやや下に緑色で塗りつぶされたより正円に近い丸があり、すぐ上にレンゾと記されている。描かれた線は下方に続く。大きく曲がった新宮の線は、彼が愛し、彼の人生における決定的な転換点を示した国、イタリアに乗り出したことを示しているのだろう。そしてジェノヴァは、二人が最初に知り合う以前に、知らぬうちに彼らを数年にわたって結び付けた場所でもある。

私たちが参照しているデッサンは、縦向きのA4判の紙に描かれており、その時系列は上から下に向かって展開していく。そうくるとは思っていなかったこの向きは、伝統的な西洋のいかなるモデルにも従っていない。おそらく、上から下の向きでも読み、直線的なもののさまざまな方向展開に慣れている日本人の鑑賞者にとっては、並外れて変わったことではないだろう。

スタジオ・アッズーロ　ラウラ・マルコリーニ

During the first meeting to discuss the exhibition, Renzo Piano produced one of his instantaneous, succinct, and illuminating drawings. It was a portrait-format drawing consisting of two lines, which were definitely not straight. They wavered, but had a consistent direction. The two paths were like separate rails, but they were rails that no train could ever run along. They wavered because no lives follow straight paths, and no matter how closely paired they are, it is beyond the bounds of possibility that the two would always remain equidistant from each other. Susumu Shingu's line starts a little higher up the sheet of paper than Piano's, with a heart-like circle filled with orange, while the other starts with a nearly regular circle filled with green, and the name Renzo written immediately above it. The lines run down the page. Shingu's line bends greatly at one point, probably indicating his adventures in Italy, a country that he came to love, which were a definitive turning point in his life. And at Genoa, without realizing it, they were joined together for several years, before they met each other.

The drawing described here is on A4 portrait paper, with the timeline running from top to bottom. That is unconventional, not following any models from the Western tradition. Nevertheless, it will probably not seem particularly strange to Japanese observers familiar with reading from top to bottom, and familiar with lines progressing in a number of directions.

Studio Azzurro　Laura Marcolini

Collaborations 01 [イタリア、ジェノヴァ Genoa, Italy]

コロンブスの風 *Columbus's Wind* 1992

ジェノヴァ港再開発 1985-2001
Re-development of the Genoa Old Harbour

Client: City of Genoa + Porto Antico SpA
Renzo Piano Building Workshop, architects
Phase One (Columbus International Exposition), 1985-92
Design team: S. Ishida (partner), E. Baglietto, G. Bianchi, M. Carroll,
O. De Nooyer, G. Grandi, D. Hart, C. Manfreddo, R. V. Truffelli (architects
in charge) with P. Bodega, V. Tolu and A. Arancio, M. Cucinella, G. Fascioli,
E. L. Hegerl, M. Mallamaci, G. McMahon, M. Michelotti, A. Pierandrei,
F. Pierandrei, S. Smith, R. Venelli, L. Vercelli and F. Doria, M. Giacomelli,
S. Lanzon, B. Merello, M. Nouvion, G. Robotti, A. Savioli; S. D'Atri, S. De Leo,
G. Langasco, P. Persia (CAD Operators); D. Lavagna (models)
Consultants: Ove Arup & Partners (structural engineering for the
Bigo); L. Mascia/D. Mascia, P. Costa, L. Lembo, V. Nascimbene,
B. Ballerini, G. Malcangi, Sidercard, M. Testone, G. F. Visconti (other
structures); Manens Intertecnica (building services); STED (cost
consultant); D. Commins (acoustics); Scene (stage equipment);
P. Castiglioni (lighting); M. Semino (supervisor of historic areas
and buildings); Cambridge Seven Associates (aquarium consultant);
Cetena (naval engineer); Origoni & Steiner (graphics); L. Moni
(site supervision)
Curator for the Italian Pavilion exhibition: G. Macchi
Wind sculptures: S. Shingu
General contractor and Project Manager: Italimpianti
Phase Two, 1993-2001
Design team: D. Hart, R. V. Truffelli (partners in charge), D. Piano with
M. Carroll, S. Ishida (partners), G. Chimeri, F. De Cillia, D. Magnano,
C. Pigionanti, V. Tolu, D. Vespier and M. Nouvion, M. Piazza, F. Santolini;
G. Langasco, M. Ottonello (CAD Operators); S. Rossi (model maker)
Consultants: Ove Arup & Partners (services engineering and
environmental studies for the Bolla); Rocca-Bacci & Associati,
E. Lora (other building services); Polar Glassin System (structural
engineering for the Bolla); B. Ballerini (other structures); STED,
Austin Italia, Tekne (cost consultants); M. Gronda (naval engineer);
P. Nalin (roads and infrastructure); Studio Galli
(sewerage networks); P. Castiglioni (lighting); G. Marini, C. Manfreddo
(fire prevention); P. Varratta (graphic design); Techint (consulting
executive architect)

Collaborations 02 [日本、大阪 Osaka, Japan]

はてしない空 *Boundless Sky* 1994

関西国際空港旅客ターミナルビル 1988-1994
Kansai International Airport Passenger Terminal Building

Client: Kansai International Airport Co. Ltd.
Renzo Piano Building Workshop, architects – N. Okabe, senior
partner in charge
in association with Nikken Sekkei Ltd., Aéroports de Paris, Japan
Airport Consultants Inc.
Competition, 1988
Design team: J. F. Blassel, R. Brennan, A. Chaaya, L. Couton, R. Keiser,
L. Koenig, K. McBryde, S. Planchez, R. Rolland, G. Torre, O. Touraine with
G. le Breton, M. Henry, J. Lelay, A. O' Carroll, M. Salerno, A. H. Téménidès,
N. Westphal
Consultants: Ove Arup & Partners (structure and services); M. Desvigne
(landscaping)
Basic design and detail design phases, 1989-1991
Design team: J. F. Blassel, A. Chavela, I. Corte, K. Fraser, R. S. Garlipp,
M. Goerd, G. Hall, K. Hirano, A. Ikegami, S. Ishida (partner), A. Johnson,
C. Kelly, T. Kimura, S. Larsen, J. Lelay, K. McBryde, T. Miyazaki, S. Nakaya,

N. Takata, T. Tomuro, O. Touraine, M. Turpin, M. Yamada, H. Yamaguchi,
T. Yamaguchi with A. Autin, G. Cohen, A. Golzari, B. Gunning, G.
Hastrich, M. Horie, I. Kubo, S. Medio, K. Miyake, S. Montaldo, S. Mukai,
K. A. Naderi, S. Oehler, T. O'Sullivan, P. Persia, F. Pierandrei, M. Rossato,
R. Shields, T. Takagawa, T. Ueno, K. Uezono, J. M. Weill, T. Yamakoshi
Consultants: Ove Arup & Partners (structure and services); Peutz &
Associés (acoustics);
R. J. Van Santen (facades); David Langdon & Everest, Futaba Quantity
Surveying Co. Ltd. (cost control); K. Nyunt (landscaping)
Construction phase, 1991-1994
Design team: A. Ikegami, T. Kimura, T. Tomuro, Y. Ueno with S. Kano,
A. Shimizu
Consultants: RFR (facades); Toshi Keikan Sekkei Inc. (canyon)
Sculpture: S. Shingu

Collaborations 03 [イタリア、トリノ Turin, Italy]

雨の軌跡 *Locus of Rain* 1995

リンゴット工場再開発計画 1983-2003
Lingotto Factory Conversion

Renzo Piano Building Workshop, architects
Competition, 1983
Client: Fiat S. p. A.
Design team: S. Ishida (associate), C. Di Bartolo, O. Di Blasi, M. Carroll,
F. Doria, G. Fascioli, E. Frigerio, R. Gaggero, D. Hart, P. Terbuchte,
R. V. Truffelli
Design Development and Construction phase, 1991-2003
Clients: Lingotto S. p. A. + Pathé + Palazzo Grassi
Design team: M. Carroll, M. Cucinella, S. Ishida, B. Plattner,
A. Belvedere, M. Salerno, S. Scarabicchi, R. V. Truffelli, M. van der
Staay, M. Varratta, P. Vincent (partners, partners and architects in
charge), A. Belvedere, M. Cattaneo, D. Piano, M. Pimmel with
P. Ackermann, A. Alborghetti, E. Baglietto (partner), L. Berellini,
A. Calafati, A. Carisetto, G. Cohen, F. Colle, P. Costa, S. De Leo,
A. De Luca, D. Dorell, S. Durr, F. Florena, K. Fraser, A. Giovannoni,
C. Hays, G. ernandez, C. Herrin, W. Kestel, P. Maggiora, D. Magnano,
M. Mariani, K. A. Naderi, T. Nguyên, T. O'Sullivan, M. Parravicini,
A. Piancastelli, M. Rossato Piano, A. Sacchi, P. Sanso, A. Stadlmayer,
A. H. Temenides, K. Van Casteren, N. Van Oosten, H. Yamaguchi
and S. Arecco, F. Bartolomeo, M. Busk-Petersen, N. Camerada,
M. Carletti, I. Cuppone, R. Croce Bermondi, B. Lenz, L. Micucci,
M. Nouvion, P. Pedrini, M. Piano; I. Corte, D. Guerrisi, G. Langasco,
L. Siracusa (CAD Operators); D. Cavagna, O. Aubert, C. Colson,
P. Furnemont, Y. Kyrkos (models)
Consultants: Ove Arup & Partners, AI Engineering, Fiat
Engineering (structure and services), Manens Intertecnica
(services/movie theater), Prodim + Teksystem (services/dental
school); Arup Acoustics, Müller BBM, Peutz & Associés
(acoustics); PI Greco Engineering (fire prevention); Davis
Langdon Everest, Fiat Engineering, GEC Ingénierie (cost control);
Emmer Pfenninger Partner (façade engineering/car engineering
school); RFR (roof structure/art gallery); Techplan (theater
equipment); P. Castiglioni (lighting); P. L. Cerri, ECO S. p. A.
(graphic design); F. Santolini, F. Mirenzi (interiors/hotel); CIA
(interiors/shopping center); Studio Vitone & Associati, F. Levi/
G. Mottino, Studio Rousset (site supervision)
Sculpture: S. Shingu

Collaborations 04 [イタリア、ジェノヴァ Genoa, Italy]

海の響き *Resonance of the Sea* 1995

レンゾ・ピアノ・ビルディング・ワークショップ　　　　1989-1991
Renzo Piano Building Workshop

Client: Renzo Piano Building Workshop
Renzo Piano Building Workshop, architects
Design team: M.Cattaneo (architect in charge), S.Ishida (partner),
M.Lusetti, F.Marano, M.Nouvion with M.Carroll, O.Di Blasi,
R.V.Truffelli, M.Varratta and D.Cavagna (models)
Consultants: A.Bellini, L.Gattoronchieri (soil engineers); P.Costa
(structure); M.Desvigne (landscaping); E.Trabella (planting);
C.Di Bartolo (bionic research)
Sculpture: S.Shingu

Collaborations 05　　　　　　　　［イタリア、レッコ Lecco, Italy］

雲との対話　*Dialogue with Clouds*　　　　　　　1998

メリディアーナ・センター　　　　　　　　　　1988-1999
Meridiana Shopping Center and Offices

Lecco (Como), Italy
Client: Camera di commercio
Colombo Costruzioni SpA
Renzo Piano Building Workshop, architects
Design team: G.Grandi (partner in charge) with S.Ishida (partner),
P.Bodega, V.Di Turi, C.Manfreddo, F.Santolini, S.Schäfer, M.Varratta
and A.Bordoni, C.Tiberti; I.Corte, S.D'Atri (CAD Operators)

Collaborations 06　　　　　　　　［イタリア、ローディ Lodi, Italy］

水の花　*Water Flower*　　　　　　　　　　　1999

バンカ・ポポラーレ・ディ・ローディ　　　　　　1991-2001
Banca Popolare di Lodi

Client: Banca Popolare di Lodi
Renzo Piano Building Workshop, architects
Design team:
Preliminary Design, 1991–1992
G.Grandi (partner in charge), A.Alborghetti, V.Di Turi, G.Fascioli,
E.Fitzgerald, C.Hayes, P.Maggiora, C.Manfreddo, V.Tolu, A.Sacchi,
S.Schäfer with S.D'Atri, G.Langasco (Cad Operators)
Design Development and Construction Phase, 1992–2001
G.Grandi (partner in charge), D.Hart (partner), V.Di Turi with A.Alborghetti,
J.Breshears, C.Brizzolara, S.Giorgio-Marrano, M.Howard, H.Peñaranda
and S.D'Atri, G.Langasco (Cad Operators); S.Rossi (models)
Consultants: M.S.C.(structure); Manens Intertecnica (services);
Müller BBM (acoustics); Gierrevideo (audio-video equiment for
Auditorium); P.Castiglioni (lighting); P.L.Cerri (graphic design);
F.Santolini (interiors)
Sculpture: S.Shingu

Collaborations 07　　　　　　　　［日本、東京 Tokyo, Japan］

宇宙に捧ぐ　*Hommage au Cosmos*　　　　　　2001

銀座メゾンエルメス　*Ginza Maison Hermès*　1998-2006
Client: Hermès Japon
Renzo Piano Building Workshop, architects
in collaboration with Rena Dumas Architecture Intérieure (Paris)
Phase One, 1998-2001
Design team: P.Vincent (partner in charge), L.Couton with G.Ducci,

P.Hendier, S.Ishida (partner), F.La Rivière and C.Kuntz; C.Colson,
Y.Kyrkos (models)
Consulting executive architect: Takenaka Corporation Design
Department
Consultants: Ove Arup & Partners (structure and services); Syllabus
(cost control); Delphi (acoustics); Ph.Almon (lighting); R.Labeyrie
(audio/video equipment); K.Tanaka (landscape); Atelier 10/N.Takata
(code research); ArchiNova Associates (site supervision)
Sculpture: S.Shingu

Collaborations 08　　　　　　　　［イタリア、ミラノ Milan, Italy］

光の雲　*Cloud of Light*　　　　　　　　　　2004

イル・ソーレ24オーレ本社　　　　　　　　　1998-2005
"Il Sole 24 Ore" Headquarters

Client: Il Sole 24 Ore SpA + Pioneer Investment Management
Renzo Piano Building Workshop, architects
Design team: A.Chaaya (partner in charge), N.Pacini with M.Cardenas,
J.Carter, G.Costa, D.Magliulo, N.Mecattaf, D.Miccolis, and J.Boon,
E.Caumont, R.Valverde; C.Colson, P.Furnemont, Y.Kyrkos
(models)
Consultants: Ove Arup & Partners + Milano Progetti (structure and
services); Progess (fire prevention); Peutz & Associés (acoustics);
R.Labeyrie (stage equipment); P.Castiglioni (lighting); E.Trabella
(planting); Origoni & Steiner (graphics); RED (cost consultant
and local consulting architect); G.Ceruti (site supervision);
M.Masnaghetti (project co-ordination)
Sculpture: S.Shingu

Collaborations 09　　　　　　　　［ギリシャ、アテネ Athens, Greece］

宇宙、叙事詩、神話　*Cosmos, Epic, Myth*　　　2016

スタヴロス・ニアルコス財団文化センター
Stavros Niarchos Foundation Cultural Center　2008-2016

Client: The Stavros Niarchos Foundation
Renzo Piano Building Workshop, architects
in collaboration with Betaplan (Athens)
Design team: G.Bianchi, V.Laffineur (partner and associate in
charge), S.Doerflinger, H.Houplain, A.Gallissian with A.Bercier,
A.Boldrini, K.Doerr, S.Drouin, G.Dubreux, S.Giorgio-Marrano,
C.Grispello, M.A.Maillard, E.Ntourlias, S.Pauletto, L.Piazza, M.Pimmel,
L.Puech and B.Brady, C.Cavo, A.Kellyie, C.Menas Porras, C.Owens,
R.Richardson; S.Moreau; O.Aubert, C.Colson and Y.Kyrkos
(models)
Consultants: Expedition Engineering/OMETE (structure); Arup/LDK
Consultants (MEP, sustainability, acoustics, lighting, security, IT);
Theater Project Consultants (theater equipment); Front (facade
engineering); Deborah Nevins & Associates/H.Pangalou
(landscaping); C&G Partners, M.Harlé/J.Cottencin (signage);
Faithful + Gould (project and cost management); AMA Alexi
Marmot Associates (library & learning space)
Sculptures: S.Shingu Y.Kyrkos (models)
Consultants: Ove Arup & Partners + Milano Progetti (structure and
services); Progess (fire prevention); Peutz & Associés (acoustics);
R.Labeyrie (stage equipment); P.Castiglioni (lighting); E.Trabella
(planting); Origoni & Steiner (graphics); RED (cost consultant and
local consulting architect); G.Ceruti (site supervision); M.Masnaghetti
(project co-ordination)
Sculpture: S.Shingu

Collaborations 10　　　　　　［アメリカ、ニューヨーク New York, USA］

虹色の葉　*Rainbow Leaves*　　　　　　　　2021

565ブルーム・ソーホー　565 Broome SoHo　2014-2019

Client: Bizzi & Partners Development
Design: Renzo Piano Building Workshop
in collaboration with SLCE Architects (New York)
Design team: E. Trezzani (partner in charge), T. Stewart (associate
in charge), J. Pauling with D. Vespier, S. Ishida, T. Wilcox and
B. Duglet; A. Pizzolato (CGI); F. Cappellini, I. Corsaro, D. Lange,
F. Terranova (models)
Consultants: RDAI (interior design); DeSimone Consulting
(structure); Ettinger Engineering Associates (MEP); ICS Mark
Pasveer (facade consultant); Balmori Associates (landscape)
Sculpture: S. Shingu

Susumu Shingu Solo Work 01　　［吹田（大阪）Suita, Osaka］

大阪万博《フローティング・サウンド》　　　　1970
Expo '70 Osaka　*Floating Sound*

Susumu Shingu Solo Work 02　［京田辺（京都）Kyotanabe, Kyoto］

雑創の森　風車・風見　　　　　　　　　　　1977
Zasso Forest School, Windmill and Wheathervane

Susumu Shingu Solo Work 03

世界巡回野外彫刻展「ウインドサーカス」　1987-1989
World Traveling Exhibition of Outdoor Sculptures, *Windcircus*

Susumu Shingu Solo Work 04

世界巡回プロジェクト「ウインドキャラバン」　2000-2001
World Traveling Project, *Wind Caravan*

Susumu Shingu Solo Work 05

「呼吸する大地（ブリージング・アース）」　　2009-
The project, *Breathing Earth*

Susumu Shingu Solo Work 06　［三田（兵庫）Sanda, Hyogo］

兵庫県立有馬富士公園「新宮晋 風のミュージアム」　2014
Arimafuji Park, "Susumu Shingu Wind Museum"

Susumu Shingu Solo Work

模型（29点）・室内作品（8点）　　　　　1981-2018
Models, Indoor Works

Susumu Shingu Future Project

地球アトリエ　　　　　　　　　　　　　　2019-
Atelier Earth

Renzo Piano Solo Work 01　　［フランス、パリ Paris, France］

ポンピドー・センター　　　　　　　　　1971-1977
Centre Georges Pompidou　　　　　　1996-2000

Client: Ministry of Cultural Affairs, Ministry of National Education
Studio Piano & Rogers, architects
Design team: R. Piano, R. Rogers, G. F. Franchini (competition,
program, interiors)
Substructure and mechanical services: W. Zbinden, H. Bysaeth,
J. Lohse, P. Merz, P. Dupont
Superstructure and mechanical services: L. Abbott, S. Ishida,
H. Naruse, H. Takahashi
Facade and galleries: E. Holt
Internal/external interfaces, audiovisual systems: A. Staton,
M. Dowd, R. Verbizh
Coordination and site supervision: B. Plattner
Environment and scenographic space: C. Brullmann
IRCAM: M. Davies, N. Okabe, K. Rupard, J. Sircus, W. Zbinden
Interiors: J. Young, F. Barat, H. Diebold, J. Fendard, J. Huc,
H. Sohlegel
Consultants: Structures and M. E. services: Ove Arup & Partners
(P. Rice, L. Grut, R. Pierce, T. Barker)
Cost control: M. Espinoza
Contractors: GTM (Jean Thaury, site engineer) (main contractor);
Krupp, Pont-à-Mousson, Pohlig (structure); Voyer (secondary
structures); Otis (elevators and escalator); Industrielle de
Chauffage, Saunier Duval (heating and ventilation); CFEM
(glazing)

1996-2000
Refurbishment of the Centre Georges Pompidou
Paris, France
Client: Centre Georges Pompidou
Renzo Piano Building Workshop, architects
Design team: P. Vincent, G. Bianchi (partners in charge), A. Gallissian
(architect in charge), N. Pacini with L. Berellini, C. Jackman,
W. Matthews, G. Modolo, J. Ruoff, A. H. Téménides and J. C. M'Fouara,
B. Piechaczyk, C. Raber, R. Valverde; C. Colson, P. Furnemont
(models)
Consultants: Gec Ingéniérie (cost control and secondary
structure); INEX (HVAC); Setec (primary structure and electrical
engineering); Peutz & Associés (acoustics); R. Labeyrie (audio/video
equipment); Integral R. Baur (signing); R. Jeol, P. Castiglioni
(lighting); Diluvial/AMCO (water basins); N. Green & A. Hunt
Associés (canopy); ODM (site co-ordinator)

Renzo Piano Solo Work 02

IBMトラベリング・パビリオン　　　　　1982-1986
IBM Traveling Pavilion

Client: IBM Europe
Renzo Piano Building Workshop, architects
Design team: S. Ishida (associate in charge), O. Di Blasi, F. Doria,
G. Fascioli, J. B. Lacoudre, N. Okabe (associate), P. Vincent, A. Traldi
Consultants: Ove Arup & Partners (P. Rice, T. Barker) (structural
and mechanical engineering)
Contractor: Calabrese Engineering S. p. a.

Renzo Piano Solo Work 03 ［ニューカレドニア、ヌメア Nouméa, New Caledonia］

チバウ文化センター　　　　　　　　　　　1991-1998
Jean-Marie Tjibaou Cultural Center

Client: Agence pour le Développement de la Culture Kanak
Renzo Piano Building Workshop, architects
Competition, 1991
Design team: P. Vincent (partner in charge), A. Chaaya (architect
in charge) with F. Pagliani, J. Moolhuijzen, W. Vassal and O. Doizy,
A. Schultz (models)
Consultants: A. Bensa (ethnologist); Desvigne & Dalnoky
(landscaping); Ove Arup & Partners (structure and ventilation);
GEC Ingénierie (cost control), Peutz & Associés (acoustics),
Scène (scenography)
Preliminary Design, 1992
Design team: P. Vincent (partner in charge), A. Chaaya, D. Rat
(architects in charge)
with J.B. Mothes A.H.Téménidès and R.Phelan, C.Catino, A.Gallissian,
R. Baumgarton, P. Darmor (models)
Consultants: A. Bensa (ethnologist); GEC Ingénierie (cost
control); Ove Arup & Partners (structural & MEP engineering
concept); CSTB (environmental studies); Agibat MTI (structure);
Scène (scenography); Peutz & Associés (acoustics); Qualiconsult
(security); Végétude (planting)
Design Development and Construction phase, 1993-1998
Design team: P. Vincent (partner in charge), D. Rat, W. Vassal
(architects in charge)
with A. El Jerari, A. Gallissian, M. Henry, C. Jackman, P. Keyser, D. Mirallie,
G. Modolo, J.B. Mothes, M. Pimmel, S. Purnama, A.H. Téménidès and
J.P. Allain (models)
Consultants: A. Bensa (ethnologist); Agibat MTI (structure); GEC
Ingénierie (MEP engineering and cost control); CSTB
(environmental studies); Philippe Délis (exhibit design); Scène
(scenography); Peutz & Associés (acoustics); Qualiconsult
(security); Végétude (planting); Intégral R. Baur (signing)

Renzo Piano Solo Work 04　　　［イギリス、ロンドン London, UK］

ザ・シャード　　　　　　　　　　　　　2000-2012
The Shard - London Bridge Tower

Client: Sellar Property Group
Renzo Piano Building Workshop, architects
in collaboration with Adamson Associates (Toronto, London)
Phase One (Planning Application), 2000-2003
Design team: J. Moolhuijzen (partner in charge), N. Mecattaf,
W. Matthews with D. Drouin, A. Eris, S. Fowler, H. Lee, J. Rousseau,
R. Stampton, M. van der Staay and K. Doerr, M. Gomes, J. Nakagawa,
K. Rottova, C. Shortle; O. Aubert, C. Colson, Y. Kyrkos (models)
Consultants: Arup (structure and services); Lerch, Bates &
Associates (vertical transportation); Broadway Malyan (consulting
architect)
Phase Two, 2004-2012Design team: J. Moolhuijzen, W. Matthews
(partner and associate in charge), B. Akkerhuis, G. Bannatyne,
E. Chen, G. Reid with O. Barthe, J. Carter, V. Delfaud, M. Durand,
E. Fitzpatrick, S. Joly, G. Longoni, C. Maxwell-Mahon, J.B. Mothes,
M. Paré, J. Rousseau, I. Tristrant, A. Vachette, J. Winrow and
O. Doule, J. Leroy, L. Petermann; O. Aubert, C. Colson, Y. Kyrkos
(models)
Consultants: WSP Cantor Seinuk (structure); Arup (building
services); Lerch, Bates & Associates (vertical transportation);
Davis Langdon (cost consultant); Townshend Architects
(landscape); Pascall + Watson (executive architect for the station)

Renzo Piano Solo Work 05　　　［フランス、パリ Paris, France］

Renzo Piano Solo Work 06　［アメリカ、ロサンゼルス Los Angeles, USA］

ジェローム・セドゥ・パテ財団　　　　　　2006-2014
Jérôme Seydoux Pathé Foundation

Client: Fondation Jérôme Seydoux - Pathé
Renzo Piano Building Workshop, architects
Design team: B. Plattner and T. Sahlmann (partner and associate
in charge) with G. Bianchi (partner), A. Pachiaudi, S. Becchi,
T. Kamp; S. Moreau, E. Ntourlias, O. Aubert, C. Colson, Y. Kyrkos
(models)
Consultants: VP Green (structure); Arnold Walz (model 3d);
Sletec (cost consultant); Inex (MEP); Tribu (sustainability); Peutz
(acoustics); Cosil (Light); Leo Berellini Architecte (interiors)

アカデミー映画博物館　　　　　　　　　2012-2020
Academy Museum of Motion Pictures

Client: Academy of Motion Picture Arts and Sciences (AMPAS)
Renzo Piano Building Workshop
in collaboration with Gensler (architect of record) and SPF:a
Design Team: M. Carroll, S. Scarabicchi (partners in charge),
L. Priano (associate in charge), D. Hammerman, J. Jones, K. Joyce
with S. Casarotto, E. Donadel, S. Ishida (partner), M. Matthews,
P. Pelanda, T. Perkins, E. Trezzani (partner) and N. Cheng,
G. Dattola, E. Ludwig, B. Ruswick, H. Travers, A. Zambrano;
B. Pignatti, A. Pizzolato (CGI); F. Cappellini, I. Corsaro, D. Lange,
F. Terranova (models)
Consultants: Buro Happold (structure, MEP); Knippers Helbig
(façade); Arup North America (theater consultant); Jaffe Holden
(acoustics, A/V); Fisher Marantz Stone (lighting); Exponent (fire/life
safety); Lerch Bates, Kiran Consulting Group, HKA Elevator
Consulting (vertical transportation); Atelier Ten (sustainability);
Simpson Gumpertz & Heger (envelope/waterproofing, building
restoration); Gibson Transportation Consulting (traffic); AECOM,
Stuart-Lynn Company (cost consultant); Walter P. Moore (interior
façade); John Fidler Preservation Technology (restoration);
Transsolar (sustainability); CS Caulkins (building maintenance);
FHT (hardware)
Project manager: Paratus Group

Renzo Piano Solo Work

アトランティス島（102点の建築作品のある架空の島）　　2018
Atlantis (The imaginary island incorporates　　(1969-2023)
scale models of all 102 of Renzo Piano's built works)

RPBW
Scale 1:1000, Model
Design team: Renzo Piano, Shunji Ishida, Andrea Malgeri
Production: Andrea Malgeri with Fausto Cappellini, Gino D'Elia,
Manzo Srl and Eugenia Dottino, Giovanna Langasco, Dimitri Lange,
Deborah Ombra, Francesco Terranova, Cristiano Zaccaria

Renzo Piano Future Project　　　　［日本、東京 Tokyo, Japan］

東京海上ビルディング　　　　　　　　　2019-
Tokio Marine Building

Client: Tokio Marine & Nichido Fire Insurance Co. Ltd.
Renzo Piano Building Workshop, architects
in collaboration with Mitsubishi Jisho Sekkei (Tokyo)
Design team: J. Moolhuijzen, A. Giralt, H. Nakatani (partners and
associate in charge)

展示作品・模型・映像
Works, Models, Videos

作品・模型・映像名 Title	制作年 Year	サイズ Size(W×D×H)cm	スケール Scale	素材 Material	分秒 Minut Second
Collaborations 01					
新宮晋《コロンブスの風》のプロトタイプ Prototype of Susumu Shingu, *Columbus's Wind*	—	15.0×33.0×46.0	—	木、金属 wood, metal	—
新宮晋《コロンブスの風》のプロトタイプ Prototype of Susumu Shingu, *Columbus's Wind*	—	18.0×18.0×52.0	—	金属、布 metal, cloth	—
ジェノヴァ港再開発全体模型 Rihabilitation of the Old Genoa harbour Bigo e Piazza delle feste - General model	1992	86.0×62.0×28.0	1:50	木、プレキシガラス wood, plexiglass	—
スタジオ・アッズーロ《平行人生》 (《コロンブスの風》+ジェノヴァ港再開発) Studio Azzurro, *Parallel Lives : Columbus's Wind* + *Re-development of the Genoa Old Harbour*	2023	—	—	—	2分20秒 2m20s
Collaborations 02					
新宮晋《はてしない空》のプロトタイプ Prototype of Susumu Shingu, *Boundless Sky*	1992	180.0×65.0×18.0	1:1	紙、金属 paper, metal	—
新宮晋《はてしない空》の模型 Model of Susumu Shingu, *Boundless Sky*	1994	261.0×272.5×300.0〜930.0	—	木、アルミニウム、ステンレス、 ポリエステル、布 wood, aluminium, stainless, polyester, cloth	—
関西国際空港旅客ターミナルビル「グライダー4」 Kansai International Airport Passanger Terminal "Glider" 4	1997	820.0×84.0×20.0	1:200	木 wood	—
関西国際空港旅客ターミナルビル「ダイナソー2」 Kansai International Airport Passanger Terminal "Dinosaur" 2	1997	350.0×36.0×34.0	1:50	金属(鋼鉄、真鍮) metal(steel, brass)	—
スタジオ・アッズーロ《平行人生》 (《はてしない空》+関西国際空港旅客ターミナルビル) Studio Azzurro, *Parallel Lives : Boundless Sky* + *Kansai International Airport Passanger Terminal Building*	2023	—	—	—	3分30秒 3m30s
スタジオ・アッズーロ《平行人生》 (《はてしない空》) Studio Azzurro, *Parallel Lives : Boundless Sky*	2023	—	—	—	2分20秒 2m20s
Collaborations 04					
新宮晋《海の響き》の模型 Model of Susumu Shingu, *Resonance of the Sea*	1995	21.3×21.3×35.2	—	アルミニウム、ステンレス、木 aluminium, stainless, wood	—

作品・模型・映像名 Title	制作年 Year	サイズ Size(W×D×H)cm	スケール Scale	素材 Material	分秒 Minut Second
RPBWプンタ・ナーヴェ事務所 「島としての建築」模型 RPBW office in Punta Nave The "building as an island" model	2000	68.0×57.0×56.0	1:100	木、プレキシガラス wood, plexiglass	—
スタジオ・アッズーロ《平行人生》 (《海の響き》+RPBW office in Punta Nave) Studio Azzurro, *Parallel Lives :* *Resonance of the Sea+RPBW office in Punta Nave*	2023	—	—	—	3分30秒 3m30s
新宮晋《小さな星座》 Susumu Shingu, *Small Constellation*	1991	53.0×45.9×31.0	1:1	ステンレス、コールテン鋼 stainless steel, corten steel	—

Collaborations 06

バンカ・ポポラーレ・ディ・ローディ全体模型 Banca Popolare di Lodi General Building Model	1999	142.5×52.5×15.5	1:200	木、プレキシガラス wood, plexiglass	—
スタジオ・アッズーロ《平行人生》 (《水の花》+バンカ・ポポラーレ・ディ・ローディ) Studio Azzurro, *Parallel Lives :* *Water Flower+Banca Popolare di Lodi*	2023	—	—	—	3分30秒 3m30s

Collaborations 07

銀座メゾンエルメス全体模型(地層階含) Ginza Maison Hermès General Building Section with Underground	1999	55.0×11.0×64.0	1:100	木、金属、プレキシガラス wood, metal, plexiglass	—
新宮晋《宇宙に捧ぐ》 Susumu Shingu, *Hommage au Cosmos*	2001	30.0×30.0×241.0	1:20	アルミニウム、ステンレス、木 aluminium, stainless, wood	—
スタジオ・アッズーロ《平行人生》 (《宇宙に捧ぐ》+銀座メゾンエルメス) Studio Azzurro, *Parallel Lives :* *Hommage au Cosmos+Ginza Maison Hermès*	2023	—	—	—	3分30秒 3m30s

Collaborations 09

スタヴロス・ニアルコス財団文化センター ランドスケープ・コンセプト Stavros Niarchos Foundation Cultural Center Landscaping Concept	2017	70.0×35.0×5.0	1:1000	紙、ウレタンスポンジ paper, schiuma	—
新宮晋《宇宙》 Susumu Shingu, *Cosmos*	2016	40.0×40.0×53.0	1:20	アルミニウム、ステンレス、木 aluminium, stainless, wood	—
スタジオ・アッズーロ《平行人生》 (《宇宙、叙事詩、神話》+ スタヴロス・ニアルコス財団文化センター) Studio Azzurro, *Parallel Lives : Cosmos, Epic, Myth+* *Stavros Niarchos Foundation Cultural Center*	2023	—	—	—	3分30秒 3m30s

作品・模型・映像名 Title	制作年 Year	サイズ Size(W×D×H)cm	スケール Scale	素材 Material	分秒 Minut Second
スタジオ・アッズーロ《平行人生》 (《宇宙、叙事詩、神話》) Studio Azzurro, *Parallel Lives* : *Cosmos, Epic, Myth*	2023	—	—	—	2分20秒 2m20s
Collaborations 10					
565ブルーム・ソーホー全体模型 565 Broome SoHo Genaral Model	—	76.2×68.6×94.0	1:100	紙、プラスチック paper, plastic	—
新宮晋《虹色の葉》の模型 Susumu Shingu, *Rainbow Leaves* Model	2021	30.0×42.0×99.0	1:100	アルミニウム、ステンレス、木 aluminium, stainless, wood	—
スタジオ・アッズーロ《平行人生》 (《虹色の葉》+565ブルーム・ソーホー Studio Azzurro, *Parallel Lives* : *Rainbow Leaves* + 565 Broome SoHo	2023	—	—	—	3分30秒 3m30s
Renzo Piano Solo Work 01					
ポンピドー・センター 「ガーベレット」梁の模型 Centre Georges Pompidou Gerberette Beam Model	1997	100.0×18.0×19.5	1:7	木 wood	—
スタジオ・アッズーロ《平行人生》 (ポンピドー・センター) Studio Azzurro, *Parallel Lives* : *Centre Georges Pompidou*	2023	—	—	—	3分30秒 3m30s
Renzo Piano Solo Work 02					
IBMトラベリング・パビリオン全体模型 IBM Travelling Pavilion General Building Model	1983	30.0×105.0×20.0	1:50	木、プレキシガラス、金属 wood, plexiglass, metal	—
スタジオ・アッズーロ《平行人生》 (IBMトラベリング・パビリオン) Studio Azzurro, *Parallel Lives* : *IBM Travelling Pavilion*	2023	—	—	—	3分30秒 3m30s
Renzo Piano Solo Work 03					
チバウ文化センター「カーズ」の発展 ―試作模型 Jean-Marie Tjibaou Cultural Center Evolution de la Case - Maquette d'étude	1995	64.0×64.0×118.0	1:20	木、金属 wood, metal	—
スタジオ・アッズーロ《平行人生》 (チバウ文化センター) Studio Azzurro, *Parallel Lives* : *Jean-Marie Tjibaou Cultural Center*	2023	—	—	—	3分30秒 3m30s

作品・模型・映像名 Title	制作年 Year	サイズ Size(W×D×H)cm	スケール Scale	素材 Material	分秒 Minut Second
Renzo Piano Solo Work 04					
ザ・シャード-ロンドン・ブリッジ・タワー 公表時のプレゼンテーション・モデル The Shard - London Bridge Tower Presentation Model - Public Inquiry	2003	23.0×23.0×63.0	1:500	プレキシガラス plexiglass	—
スタジオ・アッズーロ《平行人生》 (ザ・シャード) Studio Azzurro, *Parallel Lives : The Shard*	2023	—	—	—	3分30秒 3m30s
Renzo Piano Solo Work 05					
ジェローム・セドゥ・パテ財団 「殻」の試作のある敷地模型 Pathé Foundation Maquette du site avec étude coque	2008	48.0×57.5×21.0	1:200	木、金属 wood, metal	—
スタジオ・アッズーロ《平行人生》 (ジェローム・セドゥ・パテ財団) Studio Azzurro, *Parallel Lives :* *Jérôme Seydoux Pathé Foundation*	2023	—	—	—	3分30秒 3m30s
Renzo Piano Solo Work 06					
アカデミー映画博物館 ゲッフェン・シアターのコンセプト模型 Academy Museum of Motion Pictures Geffen Theater Conceptual Model	2013	20.0×20.0×20.0	1:200	プラスチック plastic	—
スタジオ・アッズーロ《平行人生》 (アカデミー映画博物館) Studio Azzurro, *Parallel Lives :* *Academy Museum of Motion Pictures*	2023	—	—	—	3分30秒 3m30s
Renzo Piano Future Project					
東京海上ビルディングの敷地模型 Tokio Marine Building Wood Model	2019	108.0×84.0×25.0	1:1000	木 wood	—
東京海上ビルディングのコンセプト模型 Tokio Marine Building Conceptual Model	—	23.5×23.5×22.5	1:500	木、プレキシガラス wood, plexiglass	—
東京海上ビルディングの最終模型 Tokio Marine Building Final Model	—	32.0×32.0×24.0	1:500	木、プレキシガラス wood, plexiglass	—
スタジオ・アッズーロ《平行人生》 (東京海上ビルディング) Studio Azzurro, *Parallel Lives :* *Tokio Marine Building*	2023	—	—	—	3分30秒 3m30s

主要参考文献　Main Referance

565 Broom SoHo: Residences by Renzo Piano Building Workshop, Rizzoli, 2021.

Renzo Piano: The Art of Making Buildings, Royal Academy of Arts, 2018.

Renzo Piano. Progetti d'acqua: Messa in scena di Studio Azzurro, Progetti di Renzo Piano Building Workshop, Fondazione Emilio e Annabianca Vedova, 2018.

Lorenzo Ciccarelli, Renzo Piano prima di Renzo Piano: Masters and Beginnings, Quodibet srl, 2017.

Renzo Piano, Renzo Piano: The Complete Logbook 1966-2016, Thames&Hudson, 2016.

Renzo Piano, Atene: Stavros Niarchos Foundation Cultural Center, Fondazione Renzo Piano, 2016.

新宮晋『ぼくの頭の中　INSIDE MY THINKING』株式会社ブレーンセンター、2013年

レンゾ・ピアノ著、石田俊二監修『レンゾ・ピアノ　航海日誌』TOTO出版、1998年

Renzo Piano, Giornale di Bordo, Passigli Editori, 1997.

『翔べ世界へ─ 関西国際空港株式会社10年史』関西国際空港株式会社、1995年

『CONSTRUCTION of the KANSAI INTERNATIONAL AIRPORT PASSENGER TERMINAL BUILDING』関西国際空港株式会社建設事務所建築課、1995年

『関西国際空港旅客ターミナルビル　レンゾ・ピアノ・ビルディング・ワークショップ』講談社、1994年

『汗が夢色に輝いた ── 関西国際空港建設の全記録』日刊建設工業新聞社、1994年

『AIRPORT REVIEW 関西国際空港開港記念特集』No. 90、国際空港ニュース社、1994年

Renzo Piano Building Workshop: Exhibit Design, Edizioni Lybra Immagini, 1992.

『レンゾ・ピアノ展　テーマ：環境としての建築─自然とテクノロジーの共存─』池袋サンシャインシティ文化会館他、1989年

Massimo Dini, Renzo Piano: Projets et architectures 1964-1983, Electa, 1983.

謝辞　Acknowledgements

本展の開催にあたり、新宮晋様、レンゾ・ピアノ様には、格段のご厚情を賜りました。
厚く御礼申し上げます。また、さまざまな面で貴重なご協力を賜りました皆様に深く感謝申し上げます。

We are deeply grateful to Susumu Shingu and Renzo Piano for their kindness and
understanding with regard to this exhibition.
The exhibition also benefited greatly from the invaluable cooperation of the many other people involved.
We would like to express our heartfelt gratitude to each and every one of you.

展覧会情報　Exhibition Information

本書は「Parallel Lives 平行人生 − 新宮晋＋レンゾ・ピアノ」展の公式図録として刊行されました。
This book was published as the official catalogue of the exhibition *Parallel Lives – Susumu Shingu + Renzo Piano*.

Parallel Lives 平行人生 − 新宮晋＋レンゾ・ピアノ

2023年7月13日(木)〜9月14日(木)
会場：大阪中之島美術館 5F展示室

主催
大阪中之島美術館
朝日放送テレビ
日本経済新聞社

協賛
エルメスジャポン株式会社

協力
イタリア文化会館-大阪　　Zentis Osaka
関西エアポート株式会社　　株式会社脇プロセス

後援
在大阪イタリア総領事館

展示構成
新宮晋、ステファニア・カンタ(RPBW)、石田俊二(RPBW)、スタジオ・
アッズーロ(ファビオ・チリフィーノ、ラウラ・マルコリーニ、ダニエレ・デ・パルマ、
ミケランジェロ・サンジョルジ：マルチメディアデザイン、プロジェクトディレク
ション｜マルティーナ・ローザ、シルヴィア・ペッリッツァーリ：ビデオ編集、
ポストプロダクション｜トンマーゾ・レッディ、アルベルト・モレッリ：音楽、
サウンドデザイン withフランコ・パッラヴィチーニ：オーディオレコーディ
ング｜マルゲリータ・チーティ、ソフィア・メラーティ：3Dシミュレーション協力)

展示デザイン
三木健　犬山蓉子　佐藤健
(三木健デザイン事務所)

展示協力
新宮保子　今村巌　植田ユミ　寺嶋穣二　吉井颯汰　土田有里奈(新宮アトリエ)
山形一生

展示作品レジストラー
キアーラ・ベンナーティ(FRP)　吉井颯汰(新宮アトリエ)

企画協力
前波豊(株式会社ヘミングウェイ)　mihoproject 武智美保

模型制作
アンドレーア・マルゲーリ(RPBW)　今村巌(新宮アトリエ)

企画・展覧会担当　　　　　展覧会担当
平井直子(大阪中之島美術館)　大下裕司(大阪中之島美術館)

出展作品資料所蔵者
新宮アトリエ
レンゾ・ピアノ・ビルディング・ワークショップ
フォンダツィオーネ・レンゾ・ピアノ
ビッツィ・アンド・パートナーズ

Parallel Lives – Susumu Shingu + Renzo Piano

July 13 – September 14, 2023
Venue：Nakanoshima Museum of Art, Osaka, 5F Exhibition Galleries

Organizers
Nakanoshima Museum of Art, Osaka
Asahi Television Broadcasting Corporation
Nikkei Inc.

Sponsor
Hermès Japon Co., Ltd

Cooperation
Italian Cultural Institute in Osaka　　Zentis Osaka
Kansai Airports　　waki process inc.

Support
Consulate General of Italy in Osaka

Exhibition planning
Susumu Shingu, Stefania Canta (RPBW), Shunji Ishida (RPBW),
Studio Azzurro (Fabio Cirifino, Laura Marcolini, Daniele De
Palma and Michelangelo Sangiorgi multimedia design and project
direction; Martina Rosa and Silvia Pellizzari editing and
postproduction video; Tommaso Leddi and Alberto Morelli music
and sound design with Franco Parravicini for audio recording;
Margherita Citi and Sofia Merati collaboration on 3D simulation)

Exhibition design
Ken Miki, Yoko Inuyama, Takeshi Sato
(Ken Miki & Associates)

Exhibition cooperation
Yasuko Shingu, Iwao Imamura, Yumi Ueda, Joji Terashima,
Sota Yoshii, Yurina Tsuchida (Shingu Atelier Co., Ltd.)
Issei Yamagata

Archives / Registrar
Chiara Bennati (FRP), Sota Yoshii (Shingu Atelier Co., Ltd.)

Cooperation in planning
Yutaka Maenami (Hemingway Inc.), mihoproject miho takechi

Modelmaker
Andrea Malgeri (RPBW), Iwao Imamura (Shingu Atelier Co., Ltd.)

Curator
Naoko Hirai, assisted by Yuji Oshita (Nakanoshima Museum of Art, Osaka)

Exhibits and materials provided by:
Shingu Atelier
Renzo Piano Building Workshop
Fondazione Renzo Piano
Bizzi&Partners

企画・執筆・編集	Concept, Writing and Editing
平井直子 (大阪中之島美術館)	Naoko Hirai (Nakanoshima Museum of Art, Osaka)
アートディレクション	Art Direction
三木健	Ken Miki
デザイン	Design
三木健 犬山蓉子 佐藤健	Ken Miki, Yoko Inuyama, Takeshi Sato
(三木健デザイン事務所)	(Ken Miki & Associates)
取材・執筆	Interview and Writing
前波豊 (株式会社ヘミングウェイ)	Yutaka Maenami (Hemingway Inc.)
編集協力	Editorial cooperation
石田俊二 ステファニア・カンタ (RPBW)	Shunji Ishida, Stefania Canta (RPBW)
スタジオ・アッズーロ	Studio Azzurro
新宮保子 吉井颯汰 (新宮アトリエ)	Yasuko Shingu, Sota Yoshii (Shingu Atelier Co., Ltd.)
協力	Cooperation
イタリア文化会館-大阪	Italian Cultural Institute in Osaka
日英翻訳	English and Japanese translation
有限会社フォンテーヌ	Fontaine Limited.
伊日翻訳	Italian and Japanese translation
城崎有沙	Arisa Jozaki
伊英翻訳協力	Italian and English translation (cooperation)
アンドレア・デ・アントーニ	Andrea De Antoni
英訳協力	English editing (cooperation)
スティーヴ・ディスキン	Steve Diskin
編集	Editing
福岡優子 (青幻舎)	Yuko Fukuoka (Seigensha)

平行人生 Parallel Lives

新宮 晋＋レンゾ・ピアノ Susumu Shingu + Renzo Piano

発行日	First Edition
2023年8月20日 初版発行	August 20, 2023
著者	Author
新宮 晋＋レンゾ・ピアノ	Susumu Shingu + Renzo Piano
発行者	Publisher
片山誠	Makoto Katayama
発行所	Published by
株式会社青幻舎	Seigensha Art Publishing, Inc.
〒604-8136 京都市中京区梅忠町9-1	9-1 Umetada-cho, Nakagyo-ku, Kyoto 604-8136, Japan
TEL 075-252-6766 FAX 075-252-6770	TEL +81-75-252-6766 FAX +81-75-252-6770
https:// www.seigensha.com	https:// www.seigensha.com
印刷・製本	Printed and Bound by
株式会社サンエムカラー	SunM Color Co., Ltd.